HOW TO DEAL WITH ANCESTRAL SPIRITS AND GENERATIONAL CURSES

FELICIA IFY ONWUDIWE-CHIDIKE

All scripture quotations, unless otherwise indicated, are taken from the Holy Bible, New International Version®, NIV®. Copyright ©1973, 1978, 1984, 2011 by Biblica, Inc.™ Used by permission of Zondervan. All rights reserved worldwide. www.zondervan.com The "NIV" and "New International Version" are trademarks registered in the United States Patent and Trademark Office by Biblica, Inc.™

ISBN: 978-0-9575765-5-1

How to Deal with Ancestral Spirits and Generational Curses
Copyright © 2013 Felicia Ify Onwudiwe-Chidike

Faith Revival Ministry International
52 Lovelace Road
London
SE21 8JR
Tel: +44 (0) 208 671 3080
E-mail: rev.feliciachidike@yahoo.co.uk
Website: www.faithrevivalministriesinternational.org

Re-Published by
The Vine Media Communications Ltd
Web: www.thevinemedia.co.uk

Copies available at leading bookshops nationwide.

Printed in the United Kingdom

All rights reserved. No part of this publication may be reproduced, stored in a retrieval system, or transmitted in any form or by any means, electronic, mechanical, photocopying, recording or otherwise, without the prior permission of the author.

Acknowledgement

How to Deal with Ancestral Spirits and Generational Curses is dedicated to my friend, the Holy Spirit, who gave me the inspiration to write this book and to all the people who have been affected by generational problems caused by ancestral ignorance in the practice of idolatry and worship of spirits.

Many books have been written on blessings and curses, but this text has been revealed to me by God and He wishes that all his children be delivered as they read this book and understand that God loves them. Great testimonies and instances of deliverance have been explored in this book to help those who would not otherwise submit themselves for deliverance. God is no respecter of persons.

The Bible is the only authoritative source in understanding what happens in the spirit realm and how to fight against controlling powers and defeat them. My utmost aim in writing this book is so that people will be made aware that most of their problems are caused by invisible forces that cannot be seen.

The atonement of the cross through the death and resurrection of Jesus Christ our Lord has overcome every power of the enemy.

CONTENTS

ACKNOWLEDGEMENT 3
OPENING PRAYER 7

INTRODUCTION: 9
The Importance of Your Family Tree

CHAPTER 1: 15
How to Deal with Ancestral Spirits and Generational Curses

CHAPTER 2: 31
Familiar Spirits

CHAPTER 3: 45
Generational Curses

CHAPTER 4: 61
More about Generational Curses

CHAPTER 5: 77
Some Solutions in Dealing with Ancestral or Familiar Spirits

CHAPTER 6: 89
How to Deal with the Confusion Caused by
Ancestral and Familiar Spirits

CHAPTER 7: 99
Dreams and Visions

CHAPTER 8: 125
Oral Sex is Immoral

CHAPTER 9: 129
How to Keep and Maintain Your Deliverance

CONCLUSION 141

PRAYER OF SALVATION 149

PRAYER OF RENUNCIATION 151

AUTHOR CONTACT INFORMATION 155

OPENING PRAYER

Dear Reader,

I come with you in prayer so that, before reading this book, God Almighty will open the eyes of your understanding so that you will receive revelational knowledge as to the source of the problems that you have been encountering. The Bible tells us that the secret things belong to God, but that the things which are revealed belong to man.

Father, in the name of Jesus, I thank you for revealing to me in 1987 a dream I had at the age of six, where I had gone to the place where my family practiced idol worship and where you showed me the person that has cursed me, and had me renounce and cancel the source of my problem in Jesus' name. You are the same God who I believe will reveal the sources of every problem of every person who touches this book, all sources of their problems all the way back to when they were in their mother's womb.

In Jesus' name,
Amen.

INTRODUCTION

THE IMPORTANCE OF YOUR FAMILY TREE

Whenever a person visits the doctor they will be asked about their family's medical history. You may think that because you are born again you do not need to worry about such things, but each of us needs to look into our family tree to see what patterns of sickness, negative behaviour and generational curses are common. Once we have identified the problem we must deal with it by applying the right type of knowledge: head knowledge or revelational knowledge.

Head knowledge is what we know to be a matter of fact. But, fact is not always truth. The truth of any situation can only be found in the word of God. Thus, head knowledge will *identify* a particular problem in a family, but it will not reveal the *source* of that problem.

Revelational knowledge is where God reveals the source of the problem through a vision. Once we are born again we should endeavour to enter into continuous spiritual warfare based on our revelational knowledge until the problem is dealt with and solved.

For example, my grandfather from my mother's side married seven wives and, by tradition, he only gave them land to farm. Each wife farmed her own land and looked after themselves and their own children. Each wife would provide my grandfather with food and, likewise, he would share his time between his wives. In addition, he gave a commandment that none of his daughters should be educated because they would become too wise and challenge their husbands. So he trained them to be seen and not heard.

As it happened, all my grandfather's daughters were hard working, but until their death none of them married husbands who looked after them and each of them had trained their own children. No husband even gave his wife as much as the smallest gift and curses were passed down from generation to generation, even to the granddaughters like me.

When I became born again, I had to enter into spiritual warfare because the same evil spirit that had been brought upon my mother tried to manifest itself in my life. However, my grandmother used to pray for me. She was not born again, but she used to bless me so that I would marry a good man who would look after me so that I would not go through what she went through. So you can see how the generational curse perpetuated itself: because my grandfather did not look after his wives, his daughters married husbands who did not look after their wives.

The key point to remember is that however you treat someone's child is how someone else will treat your child. Dear Reader, you must find out who sowed the bad seed in your family! Once you find the source you must uproot that bad seed.

Another example of a generational curse is the idol god (or ancestral spirit) which this same grandfather worshipped. He thought that this idol god was protecting his children, but it backfired and killed his sons until he only had two sons remaining from fifteen. Some of these sons died while he was alive, having developed a protruding stomach and then dying of some illness or another. When my grandfather died, one of his remaining sons (my uncle) inherited this idol god (or ancestral spirit). Well, you can guess what happened! My uncle only had two sons and the idol god eventually killed them both. When I was praying in England in 1998 (remember there are no barriers in the realm of the spirit), God spoke to my spirit and asked me whether I knew what had killed all my male cousins; He told me that it was the idol god that my grandfather had hanging in his living room.

I travelled to Nigeria late that year to my uncle's house and asked him if what God had told me was true. He confirmed that it was. When my uncle told me this I asked him to destroy the idol, but he told me that he would not remove it because his father had put it there. At that point I was powerless to do anything because I needed his consent before I could deal with this idol god. I left and decided not to visit this uncle anymore. At the time I had visited him the idol god had only killed one of his sons. Five months later in 1999, that idol killed the remaining son who was only in his late thirties. My uncle still refused to remove the idol. Frightened that it would kill him, he continued to do things to appease that evil spirit. So this evil spirit continued to kill and have a negative effect on the young males in the family. The only son of my grandfather, the only one of my uncles who is doing well is born again and strong in the Lord. All the others are very, very poor!

Reader, let me give you a warning at this stage: do not go uprooting idols if God has not sent you! Remember what the Bible says: "How can you enter a strong man's house and plunder his goods unless you first bind the strong man?"(Matt 12:29). If you know there is idol worship in your family, fast and pray to God for deliverance. He will use your Pastor to bring about your deliverance, but continue to renounce and cancel the work of that evil spirit. (See the prayer at the back of this book.) God spoke to my spirit recently saying, "Either make the tree good and fruit good or make the tree bad and the fruit bad."

Remember that you do not fight these battles because you are a sinner; you fight them because you are a saint. I remember that I once fell into a trance and began to see creatures that looked like ice cream cones jumping to see who could jump the highest. A voice said that Buddhists has jumped the highest, but I said 'No, Jesus has jumped the highest'. At that point a large baton came from behind and tried to hit me. God's hand appeared from nowhere and broke the baton. I heard God say, "I will break the yoke". What was my offence? Remember the blind boy in John 9, who the enemies of God wanted to kill because of his Testimony? The enemies of God wanted to kill me because of my testimony that Jesus had jumped the highest.

Be encouraged! The battles you are fighting are just the beginning and they are evidence that you are born again. God will use one person in the family to break the curse that has followed that family for generations. I had a dream on January 3, 2005, that a tree in my hometown which had been used for idol worship and sacrifices had been cut into tiny, tiny little pieces. In my spirit, I started singing the song "There is power in the blood of Jesus". When I travelled to Nigeria later in 2005, without me asking, someone told me that two sisters from my town, who went to sit at this tree from early morning until evening, had gone mental. The story is that their grandmother had done something against my family in the past. So, one month after I had been shown this tree in a dream and prayed about it, I had witnessed the work of God because the descendants of this woman (her grandmother) now go and sit at that tree.

We serve a real God, and He is a near and present help in times of need. All you have to do is call on His name in faith and He will not only deliver you, but He will deliver your children and your children's children. Once you break a generational curse it is broken forever. So read on and be delivered in the mighty name of Jesus! Amen.

CHAPTER 1

HOW TO DEAL WITH ANCESTRAL SPIRITS AND GENERATIONAL CURSES

What are Ancestral Spirits?

Ancestral spirits are the little gods our ancestors worshipped and which some people today are still worshipping. There are many little demigods. But, there is only one Almighty God, the creator of heaven and earth. He is the great I AM, the Father of our Lord Jesus Christ, the Redeemer.

A demigod, in is its most recognisable form, is an idol god in the form of shrine. People who are affected by these spirits may like to live near rivers or other natural landmarks, as they tend to worship river gods and goddess' trees or streams.

However, demigods do not just take the form of idols which are visible. A demigod can be anything we allow to take the place of God. Therefore, idol worship is not just about what we do, but about what we hold high in our hearts. Thus, idol worship can manifest itself in physical acts and also in emotional behaviour, such as anger, jealousy and bitterness. The scripture of Hebrews 12:15 tells us that bitterness defiles a person: "See to it that no one misses the grace of God and that no bitter root grows up to cause trouble and defile many."

There are some people who are addicted to plastic surgery. These people worship the way that they look and not the God who created them. If we consider the description of Rachel's beauty in Genesis 24 she had more than mere physical beauty; she held an inner beauty that could not be seen with the natural eye and it evidenced itself by the fruit of the spirit. See Galatians 5:22-23:

"But the fruit of the Spirit is love, joy, peace, forbearance, kindness, goodness, faithfulness, gentleness and self-control. Against such things there is no law."

We should worship God in spirit and in truth by exhibiting the fruit of the spirit in our daily character.

Any addiction is a form of idol worship because the person involved turns to the thing they are addicted to instead of to God. This type of idolatry can take any form: wearing a picture if your favourite pop idol on a t-shirt or covering your bedroom wall with posters, rushing to the hospital at the mere thought of illness (obsession with illness, also known as *hypochondriasis*), alcoholism, drug addiction, pornography, and the list goes on and on.

There are many examples of the operations of these evil spirits in my native Africa. In certain tribes the people will not eat certain meats because their ancestors worshipped the animals which are the source of that meat (i.e. cattle or snails); the people from that particular tribe will not eat the meat of that animal. Not because they do not like the taste, but because it is taboo in their culture. But, adhering to these unwritten rules is a form of idol worship. Even if you do not know the reason for not eating that type of meat, by abstaining you are honouring the demigod that the meat represents. When a member of a family which does this becomes born again, they might continue to abstain from eating this meat because of that learned behaviour. They acknowledge the almighty God, but deny the power thereof! Meanwhile, the Bible says that everything that God created is good and that we should bless and eat (1 Tim 4:4).

Dear Reader, I do not write this to condemn, but to bring you to a realisation of the nature of ancestral spirit and how they operate in our daily lives. Remember that the enemy of our souls is very subtle in his manifestations. Nevertheless, we need to have faith in God and live in the perfect liberty of Christ. See 1 Corinthians 6:12-20:

> [12]*"I have the right to do anything," you say – but not everything is beneficial. "I have the right to do anything" – but I will not be mastered by anything.* [13]*You say, "Food for the stomach and the stomach for food, and God will destroy them both." The body, however, is not meant for sexual immorality but for the Lord, and the Lord for the body.* [14]*By his power God raised the Lord from the dead, and he will raise us also.*
> [15]*Do you not know that your bodies are members of Christ himself? Shall I then take the members of Christ and unite them with a prostitute? Never!* [16]*Do you not know that he who unites himself with a prostitute is one with her in body? For it is said, "The two will become one flesh."* [17]*But whoever is united with the Lord is one with him in spirit.*
> [18]*Flee from sexual immorality. All other sins a person commits are outside the body, but whoever sins sexually,*

> sins against their own body. *¹⁹Do you not know that your bodies are temples of the Holy Spirit, who is in you, whom you have received from God? You are not your own; ²⁰you were bought at a price. Therefore honour God with your bodies.*

This scripture tells us that whenever a person is joined together with a harlot, they become one flesh with her. But fornication is more than a sexual act between a man and a woman, which is physical fornication. Fornication also includes not eating particular foods because of tradition, which is a type of *spiritual* fornication. Christians need to take time to find out the meaning behind the traditions they blindly follow. The reason our ancestors did not eat certain foods is because that thing was worshipped as a god or because they were married to that thing through idol worship. When the Bible says in Isaiah and Jeremiah that we go to the trees and are found naked there, it is talking about people who are married to trees through customary rights and who, therefore, commit spiritual fornication. Some people will even go to appease the spirit within the tree before getting married and perpetuate the curse in that way, passing it to their spouse. The Bible tells us that we are joined together with Christ, but through tradition Christians ignorantly follow practices which honour idols as kings and husbands. This type of idol worship can affect a person's prosperity, success and health.

The truth is that idols are nothing, but people who are entangled in idol worship because of tradition often don't know from where their tradition originated. For example, in Africa there is an outcast group of people. These people have been dedicated to serving certain idol gods and to looking after their temples. Someone, somewhere, decided that these people would have this responsibility and, as a result, these people are discriminated against. Consequently, they are not allowed to marry into the general community, so they go to other states and marry outcasts from those other areas. They have children who are also labelled outcasts and subjected to a life of discrimination, and so on and so forth. Thereby, they are creating a cycle of generational curses through idol worship.

People born into this group behave in a certain way because of the label that they have been given. These people are affected by what people say about them. In addition to this, the ancestral spirit(s) will remind these people of their family background and make them feel guilty. Remember, that it is not what people say that matters, but what you do: "For as [a man] thinks in his heart, so is he." (Pro 23:7)

Who the Son of Man sets free is free indeed. The gospel is a gospel of liberty, not of bondage. Unfortunately, oftentimes when you try to preach liberty a group of people, they will get offended and leave the Church. However, the truth is that God is not a respecter of persons and we are all equal in

CHAPTER 1: HOW TO DEAL WITH ANCESTRAL SPIRITS AND GENERATIONAL CURSES

Christ. No ancestral spirit has the right to confine a person to a life of slavery and discrimination.

Another example of this type of spiritual manipulation is reincarnation. When a person has a baby, they may visit a native doctor who will tell them that the baby is the reincarnation of a dead relative. The child will then begin to manifest the behavioural characteristics of this dead person. However, in reality what has happened is that the door has been opened for an evil spirit to affect this child's behaviour, in effect "playing out" the characteristics of the dead person to reinforce the parents' belief in reincarnation.

The purpose of this book is to set people free from any evil name that has been given to them and the evil beliefs associated with those names. The original plan of God is that man was created for worship. Isaiah 43:

> *But now, this is what the LORD says – he who created you, Jacob, he who formed you, Israel: "Do not fear, for I have redeemed you; I have summoned you by name; you are mine.*
> *²When you pass through the waters, I will be with you; and when you pass through the rivers, they will not sweep over you. When you walk through the fire, you will not be burned; the flames will not set you ablaze.*
> *³For I am the LORD your God, the Holy One of Israel, your Saviour; I give Egypt for your ransom, Cush and Seba in*

your stead.
⁴Since you are precious and honoured in my sight, and because I love you, I will give people in exchange for you, nations in exchange for your life.
⁵Do not be afraid, for I am with you; I will bring your children from the east and gather you from the west.
⁶I will say to the north, 'Give them up!' and to the south, 'Do not hold them back.' Bring my sons from afar and my daughters from the ends of the earth — ⁷Everyone who is called by my name, whom I created for my glory, whom I formed and made."
⁸Lead out those who have eyes but are blind, who have ears but are deaf.
⁹All the nations gather together and the peoples assemble. Which of their gods foretold this and proclaimed to us the former things? Let them bring in their witnesses to prove they were right, so that others may hear and say, "It is true."
¹⁰"You are my witnesses," declares the Lord, *"and my servant whom I have chosen, so that you may know and believe me and understand that I am he. Before me no god was formed, nor will there be one after me. ¹¹I, even I, am the* Lord, *and apart from me there is no saviour. ¹²I have revealed and saved and proclaimed — I, and not some foreign god among you. You are my witnesses," declares the* Lord, *"that I am God.*
¹³Yes, and from ancient days I am he. No one can deliver out of my hand. When I act, who can reverse it?"

¹⁴This is what the LORD says – your Redeemer, the Holy One of Israel: "For your sake I will send to Babylon and bring down as fugitives all the Babylonians, in the ships in which they took pride.
¹⁵I am the LORD, your Holy One, Israel's Creator, your King."
¹⁶This is what the LORD says – he who made a way through the sea, a path through the mighty waters, ¹⁷who drew out the chariots and horses, the army and reinforcements together, and they lay there, never to rise again, extinguished, snuffed out like a wick:
¹⁸ "Forget the former things; do not dwell on the past. ¹⁹See, I am doing a new thing! Now it springs up; do you not perceive it? I am making a way in the wilderness and streams in the wasteland. ²⁰The wild animals honour me, the jackals and the owls, because I provide water in the wilderness and streams in the wasteland, to give drink to my people, my chosen,²¹the people I formed for myself that they may proclaim my praise.
²²"Yet you have not called on me, Jacob, you have not wearied yourselves for me, Israel. ²³You have not brought me sheep for burnt offerings, nor honoured me with your sacrifices. I have not burdened you with grain offerings nor wearied you with demands for incense. ²⁴You have not bought any fragrant calamus for me, or lavished on me the fat of your sacrifices. But you have burdened me with your sins and wearied me with your offences.
²⁵"I, even I, am he who blots out your transgressions, for

my own sake, and remembers your sins no more. ²⁶Review the past for me, let us argue the matter together; state the case for your innocence. ²⁷Your first father sinned; those I sent to teach you rebelled against me. ²⁸So I disgraced the dignitaries of your temple; I consigned Jacob to destruction and Israel to scorn.

From the above scriptures (verses 1-8), you see how our Almighty God is prepared to help those who trust in Him. From verses 9-20, He declares the foolishness of those who worship idol gods; from 21-28, He reassures us of his Divine nature and His continuing interest in His people. We should note here that Israel/Jacob represented the Church; the Church is the spiritual Israel. Even within the nation of Israel, God separated those who obey Him from those who disobey him, and He does the same with the Churches. His blessings are concentrated on those who obey him.

The main purpose God created you and I, is so that we would give him the praise that is due to Him. How do we give God praise? The only way you can give God praise is by acknowledging all the good things that God has done in your life and the people who He has used to do such things. I would suggest that you take a pen and paper and list all the things that God has done for you. This is a positive exercise. Do not think about what you have not achieved; count all your achievements, even the little ones! Even the fact that you are alive today is a testimony and a blessing from God.

I want you to understand that the fact that you are alive today is not a result of your goodness. It is because God has spared your life because of his mighty power and love for you. It is better to be a living dog than a dead lion. I have seen wealthy people who have died and they have taken nothing with them to the grave.

People worship idol gods because of fear. However, people become engrossed in this fear because of a lack of understanding. They think their lives will be prolonged because of the sacrifices they make to the dead spirits of their forefathers. These dead spirits cannot help the living. God is alive He is not dead! This same God whom we serve raised Jesus Christ from the dead to prove that He is the God of the living and not the God of the dead. This is the reason why we who are living and on the last day we must give an account of all that we did with our time here on earth. The life that we live here on earth is temporary. The day you die you will face the judgement seat of God. If you spend your life on earth believing in dead spirits that influenced you to do evil and wicked things, then you will definitely spend the rest of eternity in hell fire where there is wailing and gnashing of teeth. God forbid! This is not your portion He intended for you, but the choice is yours.

SPIRITUAL ISRAEL

Read Romans 2:

You, therefore, have no excuse, you who pass judgment on someone else, for at whatever point you judge another, you are condemning yourself, because you who pass judgment do the same things. ²Now we know that God's judgment against those who do such things is based on truth. ³So when you, a mere human being, pass judgment on them and yet do the same things, do you think you will escape God's judgment? ⁴Or do you show contempt for the riches of his kindness, forbearance and patience, not realising that God's kindness is intended to lead you to repentance?

⁵ But because of your stubbornness and your unrepentant heart, you are storing up wrath against yourself for the day of God's wrath, when his righteous judgment will be revealed. ⁶God "will repay each person according to what they have done." ⁷To those who by persistence in doing good seek glory, honour and immortality, he will give eternal life. ⁸But for those who are self-seeking and who reject the truth and follow evil, there will be wrath and anger. ⁹There will be trouble and distress for every human being who does evil: first for the Jew, then for the Gentile; ¹⁰but glory, honour and peace for everyone who does good: first for the Jew, then for the Gentile. ¹¹For God does not show favouritism.

¹²All who sin apart from the law will also perish apart from the law, and all who sin under the law will be judged by the law. ¹³For it is not those who hear the law who are righteous in God's sight, but it is those who obey the law who will be declared righteous. ¹⁴(Indeed, when Gentiles, who do not have the law, do by nature things required by the law, they are a law for themselves, even though they do not have the law. ¹⁵They show that the requirements of the law are written on their hearts, their consciences also bearing witness, and their thoughts sometimes accusing them and at other times even defending them.) ¹⁶This will take place on the day when God judges people's secrets through Jesus Christ, as my gospel declares.

¹⁷Now you, if you call yourself a Jew; if you rely on the law and boast in God; ¹⁸if you know his will and approve of what is superior because you are instructed by the law; ¹⁹if you are convinced that you are a guide for the blind, a light for those who are in the dark, ²⁰an instructor of the foolish, a teacher of little children, because you have in the law the embodiment of knowledge and truth — ²¹you, then, who teach others, do you not teach yourself? You who preach against stealing, do you steal? ²²You who say that people should not commit adultery, do you commit adultery? You who abhor idols, do you rob temples? ²³You who boast in the law, do you dishonour God by breaking the law? ²⁴As it is written: "God's name is blasphemed among the Gentiles because of you."

²⁵Circumcision has value if you observe the law, but if you break the law, you have become as though you had not been circumcised. ²⁶*So then, if those who are not circumcised keep the law's requirements, will they not be regarded as though they were circumcised?* ²⁷*The one who is not circumcised physically and yet obeys the law will condemn you who, even though you have the written code and circumcision, are a lawbreaker.* ²⁸*A person is not a Jew who is one only outwardly, nor is circumcision merely outward and physical.* ²⁹*No, a person is a Jew who is one inwardly; and circumcision is circumcision of the heart, by the Spirit, not by the written code. Such a person's praise is not from other people, but from God.*

My beloved, we should endeavour to live a life that is pleasing to God. God sees your heart. He knows what you do both secretly and in the open. Some people struggle to please human beings, but in so doing they live a life of double standards because they are more concerned about what people think about them than what their Creator thinks. They worship the creation and not the Creator. But, you should remember this one thing: no matter how wonderfully good you are as a Christian, evil doers will hate you for being good.

Look at verses 28-29: what do they tell you about who you are? Whose praise is not of men but of God? God required more than outward evidence of Christianity and His praise relates to who you are in the spirit, and who you are in the spirit will affect how you behave in the flesh. For example, you may have come from a family with a background of idol worship but, once you do not behave in the negative way that is the result of the influence of ancestral spirit, you are free. The transformation from negative behaviour to positive behaviour will not be immediate, but as you continue to read the word of God and pray, change will surely come.

WHOSE PRAISE IS NOT OF MEN BUT OF GOD

Ancestral spirits influence people to please the flesh and to trust in themselves instead of God. Therefore, ancestral spirits cause people to operate under the influence of the flesh and to manifest the works of the flesh.
Consider Galatians 5: 19-21:

> *"The acts of the flesh are obvious: sexual immorality, impurity and debauchery; [20]idolatry and witchcraft; hatred, discord, jealousy, fits of rage, selfish ambition, dissensions, factions [21]and envy; drunkenness, orgies, and the like. I warn you, as I did before, that those who live like this will not inherit the kingdom of God."*

CHAPTER 2

FAMILIAR SPIRITS

Familiar spirits are similar to ancestral spirits. Familiar spirits are called such because they are *familiar* to certain characteristics of families, towns, cities, countries, et cetera. They have observed their *familiar* surroundings and people for years; they know what attracts them to sin. They even know the covenants the ancestors of individuals have entered into with demonic spirits. These spirits will resist an individual delivering them and casting them out to another place, because it will take them time to study new people with different characters to enable them to influence their behaviour.

For example, we read in Mark 5:1-14:

> ¹They went across the lake to the region of the Gadarenes. ²When Jesus got out of the boat, a man with an evil spirit came from the tombs to meet him. ³This man lived in the tombs, and no one could bind him any more, not even with a chain. ⁴For he had often been chained hand and foot, but he tore the chains apart and broke the irons on his feet. No one was strong enough to subdue him. ⁵Night and day among the tombs and in the hills he would cry out and cut himself with stones. ⁶When he saw Jesus from a distance, he ran and fell on his knees in front of him. ⁷He shouted at the top of his voice, "What do you want with me, Jesus, Son of the Most High God? Swear to God that you won't torture me!" ⁸For Jesus had said to him, "Come out of this man, you evil spirit!" ⁹Then Jesus asked him, "What is your name?" "My name is Legion," he replied, "for we are many." ¹⁰And he begged Jesus again and again not to send them out of the area.
> ¹¹ A large herd of pigs was feeding on the nearby hillside. ¹²The demons begged Jesus, "Send us among the pigs; allow us to go into them." ¹³He gave them permission, and the evil spirits came out and went into the pigs. The herds, about two thousand in number, rushed down the steep bank into the lake and were drowned. ¹⁴Those tending the pigs ran off and reported this in the town and countryside, and the people went out to see what had happened.

We read here the story of a man who was bound by a strong spirit. In verse 12, all the Devils besought Jesus, begging Him to send them into the swine. These are examples of familiar spirits. They do not care whether they live in human-beings or in animals, but they want to stay around the same area to monitor people's activities.

In other families, women may live under a curse generally called "ill luck" or "bad luck". They are never appreciated by their husbands no matter how kind they are to them; this "bad luck" is passed down because their fathers did not appreciate their wives. Whatever any man sows, the same he will reap. If you mistreat someone else's daughter (e.g. a husband mistreating his wife, his father-in-law's daughter) someone will do the same to yours.

Satan's number one strategy is sexual immorality. The Bible warns against that in 1Corinthians 6:15-20:

> [15]*Do you not know that your bodies are members of Christ himself? Shall I then take the members of Christ and unite them with a prostitute? Never!* [16]*Do you not know that he who unites himself with a prostitute is one with her in body? For it is said, "The two will become one flesh."* [17]*But whoever is united with the Lord is one with him in spirit.* [18]*Flee from sexual immorality. All other sins a person commits are outside the body, but whoever sins sexually, sins against their own body.* [19]*Do you not know that your*

bodies are temples of the Holy Spirit, who is in you, whom you have received from God? You are not your own; [20]*you were bought at a price. Therefore honour God with your bodies.*

Satan empowers his agents to get into sexual immorality because he knows the consequences.

A girl came to us for deliverance in 1991. She told us how she was being oppressed by a demonic husband. According to her, any man who proposed to her would immediately die. But what brought her to us was because her spirit husband had just killed her boyfriend, whom she loved dearly. Her dead boyfriend was a security guard. He left his duty to have fun with her and, during their sexual intercourse, he proposed marriage to her. After he said that, her spirit husband hit the man with a large baton. She saw the spirit husband walk into the room, but her boyfriend did not see him. Immediately the spirit husband hit her boyfriend. He screamed 'My head! Oh, my head!' The boyfriend quickly dressed up and went back to work. Later, she called to check how he was feeling because she had a suspicion that he was going to die. As they were talking, the phone went dead. She called the police to report the incident but did not tell them that the boyfriend had been to her flat. By the time the police arrived the man was dead and, because there was no evidence of physical attack, the doctors concluded that his death was due to inhalation of gas he used to heat his room. (Remember that medical doctors cannot discern spiritual matters nor do they have proper diagnosis for such things.)

I told this lady to fast with me for three days so that we could pray for her to break the curse. She told me that fasting would not be a problem but that she could not do without sex, or else the spiritual husband would kill her. She had been instructed to pass on demonic spirits to men through sexual intercourse. She was, therefore, required to indulge herself in an excessive amount of sexual activity. The conditions were that men were allowed to have sex with her but must not marry her. She was required to have sex with as many men as possible in order to transfer the demonic spirits. To get married would hinder her assignment.

When these wicked spirits are passed down through the generations there can never be peace in the family. These demons influence a person's behaviour. The works of the flesh will begin to manifest: hatred, strife, et cetera. It does not matter whether it is the man or that woman that is unfaithful. The fact is that somebody opened the door to demonic attacks on the family. The man may blame the woman, the woman may blame the man, accusing one another, but the truth is a demonic and unclean spirit is at work.

CAST OUT THE UNCLEAN SPIRITS

Matthew 10:1 says: "And when he had called unto him his twelve disciples, he gave them power against unclean spirits, to cast them out, and to heal all manner of sickness and all manner of disease. (KJV)"

The first commission given to the disciples was an assignment to cast out unclean spirits. The church must deal with unclean spirits. Anybody caught in fornication or adultery must be counselled and brought to repentance. It is a deadly spirit. It works faster than cancer or any other disease.

SATAN COMES TO KILL, STEAL, AND DESTROY

In the Bible, we read about the story of David and Bathsheba. Satan got into David's family through sexual immorality and began to steal, kill, and destroy. David's son, Ammon, stole his sister, Tamar's virginity. Ammon was then killed by his brother, Absalom, for the sin of raping their sister.

David and his family were destroyed and wounded because of the calamity that had befallen them as a result of sexual immorality. The story is recounted in 2 Samuel 13.

CONSEQUENCES OF ANCESTRAL SPIRITS

Sexual immorality can lead to unforgiveness. I have heard of three lady ministers who died of cancer because they found it difficult to forgive their husbands. Unforgiveness hinders your prayers, and if God does not hear your prayers, how can they be answered?

Consider Mark 11:12-26:

> [12] The next day as they were leaving Bethany, Jesus was hungry. [13] Seeing in the distance a fig tree in leaf, he went to find out if it had any fruit. When he reached it, he found nothing but leaves, because it was not the season for figs. [14] Then he said to the tree, "May no one ever eat fruit from you again." And his disciples heard him say it.
> [15] On reaching Jerusalem, Jesus entered the temple courts and began driving out those who were buying and selling there. He overturned the tables of the money changers and the benches of those selling doves, [16] and would not allow anyone to carry merchandise through the temple courts. [17] And as he taught them, he said, "Is it not written: 'My house will be called a house of prayer for all nations?' But you have made it 'a den of robbers.'"
> [18] The chief priests and the teachers of the law heard this and began looking for a way to kill him, for they feared him, because the whole crowd was amazed at his teaching.
> [19] When evening came Jesus and his disciples went out of

the city. ²⁰In the morning, as they went along, they saw the fig tree withered from the roots. ²¹Peter remembered and said to Jesus, "Rabbi, look! The fig tree you cursed has withered!" ²²"Have faith in God," Jesus answered. ²³"Truly, I tell you, if anyone says to this mountain, 'Go, throw yourself into the sea,' and does not doubt in their heart but believes that what they say will happen, it will be done for them.
²⁴Therefore I tell you, whatever you ask for in prayer, believe that you have received it, and it will be yours. ²⁵And when you stand praying, if you hold anything against anyone, forgive them, so that your Father in heaven may forgive you your sins."

Many people like to quote verse 24 of the above scripture by itself, but verses 25 and 26 are a continuation of verse 24. No matter how big your faith, you must endeavour to forgive those who have wronged you.

In re-reading verse 15, it says: "On reaching Jerusalem, Jesus entered the temple courts and began driving out those who were buying and selling there. He overturned the tables of the money changers and the benches of those selling doves".

YOUR BODY IS A TEMPLE

We read in 1Corinthians 3:16 that your body is the temple of the Spirit if God, and that the Spirit of God dwells in us. If any man should defile the temple of God, him shall God destroy; for the temple of God is holy, and you are God's temple.

The temple that Jesus is referring to, where things are bought and sold, is your soul. Jesus said to the people that He will not dwell any longer in a house that was made by hands. As the temple of God, what do you allow to be sold in your mind? The mind is the battle field. That is where the Devil would like to buy and sell filthy thoughts.

The main reason Satan causes a spouse to commit sin against his/her other half is because he wants the other partner to feel hurt and react in the flesh. The Devil will always remind the honest partner how much he/she has been hurt. The honest partner would probably not trust the guilty partner any longer. This reaction will breed mistrust, unforgiveness, and strife. The Devil's main purpose is not just the acts of sin but the *reactions* that sin could provoke which will eventually lead to death. Remember that Satan comes only to steal, kill, and destroy (John 10:10a). But in part B of that same verse Jesus said, 'I am come that they might have life and that they might have it more abundantly.'

You cannot have abundant life if you disobey the Word of God. The Word of God is JESUS Himself! The Bible says that Jesus is the Word that became 'flesh.' Jesus is the Shepherd and we are His sheep. Jesus said that His sheep shall hear His voice, and they shall be one fold, and one Shepherd. (John 10:16)

The Devil understands the power of unity. Therefore, he comes to cause confusion and strife. The amazing thing is that usually the wounded are the ones who get killed.

When you have been wounded, try and receive healing. It is only Jesus who can offer you that healing. If you refuse his healing process you will surely die, but that will not be your portion He intended for you in His name. Amen.

Let us look at Luke 17:1-6:
> *Jesus said to his disciples: "Things that cause people to stumble are bound to come, but woe to anyone through whom they come. ²It would be better for them to be thrown into the sea with a millstone tied around their neck than to cause one of these little ones to stumble. ³So watch yourselves.*
> *"If your brother or sister sins against you, rebuke them; and if they repent, forgive them. ⁴Even if they sin against you seven times in a day and seven times come back to you saying 'I repent,' you must forgive them."*
> *⁵The apostles said to the Lord, "Increase our faith!"*

> *⁶He replied, "If you have faith as small as a mustard seed, you can say to this mulberry tree, 'Be uprooted and planted in the sea,' and it will obey you"*

This scripture speaks for itself. Our inability to forgive will lead us to disobedience. It is only obedience that attracts God's blessing upon your life. Sometimes it is difficult to forgive when you are hurting. If this is the case, then ask the Holy Spirit to help you forgive. Faith works by love. Jesus went to the cross even when we were sinners; Christ died for the ungodly.

My brothers and sisters, you are holy temples in the Lord! Ephesians 2:21 states, "Do not allow filthy thoughts to dwell in your temple." Ephesians 2:21-22 says: "In him the whole building is joined together and rises to become a holy temple in the Lord. And in him you too are being built together to become a dwelling in which God lives by his Spirit."

When the Devil reminds you of the terrible things you are going through and how unfair those things are, rebuke him and let him know that he made the person to do the wrong or evil against you. Refuse to meditate on the evil that has been done against you because the weapons of our welfare are not carnal but mighty through God by the pulling down of strongholds (2 Corinthians 10:4).

WHY DO ANCESTRAL SPIRITS INFLUENCE PEOPLE TO DISOBEY GOD?

Disobedience goes hand in hand with curses. Deuteronomy 28:15-68 lists the curses that follow disobedience. God wants us to serve him with joy and gladness of heart, for the abundance of all things. Let's look specifically at verses 47-48.

> *⁴⁷Because you did not serve the LORD your God joyfully and gladly in the time of prosperity, ⁴⁸therefore in hunger and thirst, in nakedness and dire poverty, you will serve the enemies the LORD sends against you. He will put an iron yoke on your neck until he has destroyed you.*

These evil spirits attack Christians through associations with wicked people. The Devil will use people to offend you and, if you cannot discern the spirit behind the offence, you may start murmuring and complaining about them, thereby grieving God. It is easy to forget all the good things God has used this person to do for you in the past. All you see begin to see in them is fault and this fault-finding may lead to hatred and some other evil works. You can open the door to Satan to attack you more because of this fault-finding habit.

The epistle of 1 John 3:15 says that if a person has hatred in their heart, that person is a murderer.

The solution to the problem is to commit everything to God in prayer. The Bible says that vengeance is the Lord's. Do not allow the Devil to steal your peace! Remember John 14:1: "Let not your heart be troubled, ye who believe in God, believe also in me."

CHAPTER 3

GENERATIONAL CURSES

Curses come upon people as a result of disobedience to the word of God. See Deuteronomy 28:15-68:

> *¹⁵However, if you do not obey the L*ORD *your God and do not carefully follow all his commands and decrees I am giving you today, all these curses will come on you and overtake you:*
> *¹⁶You will be cursed in the city and cursed in the country.*
> *¹⁷Your basket and your kneading trough will be cursed.*
> *¹⁸The fruit of your womb will be cursed, and the crops of your land, and the calves of your herds and the lambs of your flocks.*
> *¹⁹You will be cursed when you come in and cursed when*

you go out.

²⁰The LORD will send on you curses, confusion and rebuke in everything you put your hand to, until you are destroyed and come to sudden ruin because of the evil you have done in forsaking him. ²¹ The LORD will plague you with diseases until he has destroyed you from the land you are entering to possess. ²²The LORD will strike you with wasting disease, with fever and inflammation, with scorching heat and drought, with blight and mildew, which will plague you until you perish. ²³The sky over your head will be bronze, the ground beneath you iron. ²⁴The LORD will turn the rain of your country into dust and powder; it will come down from the skies until you are destroyed.

²⁵The LORD will cause you to be defeated before your enemies. You will come at them from one direction but flee from them in seven, and you will become a thing of horror to all the kingdoms on earth. ²⁶Your carcasses will be food for all the birds and the wild animals, and there will be no one to frighten them away. ²⁷The LORD will afflict you with the boils of Egypt and with tumours, festering sores and the itch, from which you cannot be cured. ²⁸The LORD will afflict you with madness, blindness and confusion of mind. ²⁹At midday you will grope about like a blind person in the dark. You will be unsuccessful in everything you do; day after day you will be oppressed and robbed, with no one to rescue you.

³⁰You will be pledged to be married to a woman, but

another will take her and rape her. You will build a house, but you will not live in it. You will plant a vineyard, but you will not even begin to enjoy its fruit. ³¹*Your ox will be slaughtered before your eyes, but you will eat none of it. Your donkey will be forcibly taken from you and will not be returned. Your sheep will be given to your enemies, and no one will rescue them.* ³²*Your sons and daughters will be given to another nation, and you will wear out your eyes watching for them day after day, powerless to lift a hand.* ³³*A people that you do not know will eat what your land and labor produce, and you will have nothing but cruel oppression all your days.* ³⁴*The sights you see will drive you mad.* ³⁵*The* Lord *will afflict your knees and legs with painful boils that cannot be cured, spreading from the soles of your feet to the top of your head.*

³⁶*The* Lord *will drive you and the king you set over you to a nation unknown to you or your ancestors. There you will worship other gods, gods of wood and stone.* ³⁷*You will become a thing of horror, a byword and an object of ridicule among all the peoples where the* Lord *will drive you.*

³⁸*You will sow much seed in the field but you will harvest little, because locusts will devour it.* ³⁹*You will plant vineyards and cultivate them but you will not drink the wine or gather the grapes, because worms will eat them.* ⁴⁰*You will have olive trees throughout your country but you will not use the oil, because the olives will drop off.* ⁴¹*You will have sons and daughters but you will not keep*

them, because they will go into captivity. ⁴²Swarms of locusts will take over all your trees and the crops of your land.

⁴³The foreigners who reside among you will rise above you higher and higher, but you will sink lower and lower. ⁴⁴They will lend to you, but you will not lend to them. They will be the head, but you will be the tail.

⁴⁵All these curses will come on you. They will pursue you and overtake you until you are destroyed, because you did not obey the LORD your God and observe the commands and decrees he gave you. ⁴⁶They will be a sign and a wonder to you and your descendants forever.

⁴⁷Because you did not serve the LORD your God joyfully and gladly in the time of prosperity, ⁴⁸therefore in hunger and thirst, in nakedness and dire poverty, you will serve the enemies the LORD sends against you. He will put an iron yoke on your neck until he has destroyed you.

⁴⁹The LORD will bring a nation against you from far away, from the ends of the earth, like an eagle swooping down, a nation whose language you will not understand, ⁵⁰a fierce-looking nation without respect for the old or pity for the young. ⁵¹They will devour the young of your livestock and the crops of your land until you are destroyed. They will leave you no grain, new wine or olive oil, nor any calves of your herds or lambs of your flocks until you are ruined. ⁵²They will lay siege to all the cities throughout your land until the high fortified walls in which you trust fall down. They will besiege all the cities throughout the land the

LORD your God is giving you.
⁵³Because of the suffering your enemy will inflict on you during the siege, you will eat the fruit of the womb, the flesh of the sons and daughters the LORD your God has given you. ⁵⁴Even the most gentle and sensitive man among you will have no compassion on his own brother or the wife he loves or his surviving children, ⁵⁵and he will not give to one of them any of the flesh of his children that he is eating. It will be all he has left because of the suffering your enemy will inflict on you during the siege of all your cities. ⁵⁶The most gentle and sensitive woman among you – so sensitive and gentle that she would not venture to touch the ground with the sole of her foot – will begrudge the husband she loves and her own son or daughter, ⁵⁷the afterbirth from her womb and the children she bears. For in her dire need she intends to eat them secretly because of the suffering your enemy will inflict on you during the siege of your cities.
⁵⁸If you do not carefully follow all the words of this law, which are written in this book, and do not revere this glorious and awesome name – the LORD your God – ⁵⁹the LORD will send fearful plagues on you and your descendants, harsh and prolonged disasters, and severe and lingering illnesses. ⁶⁰He will bring on you all the diseases of Egypt that you dreaded, and they will cling to you. ⁶¹The LORD will also bring on you every kind of sickness and disaster not recorded in this Book of the Law, until you are destroyed. ⁶²You who were as numerous as

the stars in the sky will be left but few in number, because you did not obey the LORD your God. ⁶³Just as it pleased the LORD to make you prosper and increase in number, so it will please him to ruin and destroy you. You will be uprooted from the land you are entering to possess.
⁶⁴Then the LORD will scatter you among all nations, from one end of the earth to the other. There you will worship other gods – gods of wood and stone, which neither you nor your ancestors have known. ⁶⁵Among those nations you will find no repose, no resting place for the sole of your foot. There the LORD will give you an anxious mind, eyes weary with longing, and a despairing heart. ⁶⁶You will live in constant suspense, filled with dread both night and day, never sure of your life. ⁶⁷In the morning you will say, "If only it were evening!" and in the evening, "If only it were morning!" – because of the terror that will fill your hearts and the sights that your eyes will see. ⁶⁸The LORD will send you back in ships to Egypt on a journey I said you should never make again. There you will offer yourselves for sale to your enemies as male and female slaves, but no one will buy you.

I encourage you to pay particular attention to verses 47-48. I want you to pause for a minute and ask yourself whether any of the curses mentioned here run in your family. In some families the men are never satisfied with one wife, always finding fault with their wives. They make many excuses and give numerous reasons for their unfaithfulness, or end up marrying other women.

In some cases, the young women never get married on time or if they do, they will not remain in the marriage. If they try to remain they see only the man's fault and will not accord the man his due respect. In some families, they are strangers to happiness and wealth, and in wealthy families they become frustrated. They drink excessively or flirt about in pursuit of strange joy and happiness. However, there is no genuine happiness without obedience to the word of God.

In some families, the members do not appreciate one another. Their job is to criticise anyone doing well without realising that they are doing well by God's grace. They want to pull their brother or sister down because they think they are in competition with each other. They forget that God is no respecter of persons. In Romans 9:15-16, God declares His intention in respect to those He chooses to bless. It is not by a person's power or might but by the spirit of the living God: "For he says to Moses, 'I will have mercy on whom I have mercy, and I will have compassion on whom I have compassion.' It does not, therefore, depend on human desire or effort, but on God's mercy."

You need to believe in the word of God and exercise patience and faith in order to be blessed by Him (Romans 9:19-29). Generational curses run from generation to generation up to the fourth generation until somebody in the family gets to know God and decides to cancel the evil work by renunciation and, more importantly, to refuse to act and practice the evil deeds that are against the will of God. These deeds which are the result of a sinful nature are called the Works of the Flesh (Galatians 5:19-21).

You may not approve of your parents character or attitude towards people. But, when you grow up you may realise that you do the same thing. This happens as the result of the influence of the Devil. The weapons of our warfare are not carnal, but mighty through God to the pulling down of strongholds. We do not fight against flesh and blood but against principalities (2 Corinthians 10:4).

Allow me to give you a personal example: my mother was a very good woman, and that is an honest statement. She loved people. She gave her best to people but she was not a romantic person like my father. My father was the outgoing type. He was very handsome and was a British soldier who fought during the Second World War. He was in the army until 1970. My siblings and I used to ask them what kept them together in marriage because we saw that they were not compatible. My father would make hundreds of friends in a minute, whilst my mother took time to choose her friends and therefore, had fewer.

As I was growing up, people would tell me that I had my

mother's temperament. I heard this statement over and over again.

I came to England 1980 and met my husband in 1982. We got married in December of the same year by tradition and wedded in England in 1983. We were in love. I thought our problem started when we moved to London in 1985. Those problems compounded when we started running a church in 1991. Some ladies in the church began to fight about the unity my husband and I shared. Then the Devil planted the thought in my mind that the way I related to my husband was unfair to those women in the church, because many of those women did not have husbands. The Devil told me that I was making them feel bad when I held hands or kissed my husband in public.

RELIGIOUS SPIRITS

My problem began with this situation. All of my mother's behaviours began to surface in me within a twinkle of an eye. My mum had a habit of depriving herself of any type of pleasure just to please others.

Before I was married, my family and I lived on Sanusi Street in Kano. People nicknamed her "Mama Sanusi" because her house became a restaurant/hostel. I started to deny myself happiness in order to please others. People would say "like mother, like daughter", but I call it the manifestation of a religious/familiar spirit. Whenever I heard about a person's problem, I took it upon myself to pray, thinking that the problem would be solved by *my* power or how *I* interceded on their behalf.

When the Lord Jesus appeared to me in May 1987, He called me into intercession; He gave me gifts of prophecy and the gift of discerning spirits. From that time on, prayer became like breathing to me. The Devil then began to use my prayer life to hold me in bondage. The Devil accused me whenever I spent time with my husband and I began to quarrel over small issues. He also used my commitment to God to buffet others who were not as committed as I was. Despite the fact that the Lord corrected me many times, I would obey him for a while only to go back to shouting and screaming, obsessing over being "Ify the Perfectionist". I even pulled away some girls in the church from having boyfriends.

Then the Lord's assignment was to preach the Word and plead the blood and that He would cleanse them. I obeyed on a couple of occasions and then went back to trying to cleanse people myself by preaching at their mistakes. Sometimes I even suspended them from church. The problem started to get out of hand and many people left the church as a result of my behaviour.

RELIGIOUS SPIRITS LEAD TO BONDAGE

I was attacked spiritually, physically, and financially because I had opened the door to the enemy. I felt as though changing my behaviour would be a promotion of sin. I could never stop preaching the gospel of holiness and truth. However, the truth was that I needed to have compassion on those that the Devil had held captive by his will (2Timothy 2:24-26). I forgot that I had been terrible sinner before the Lord had shown me compassion.

By trying to correct others by force, I had become worse than them. Anger was my food, despite my holy prayer life. Then Jesus opened my eyes to see that I was not representing him well. I was not respecting my husband. I judged every statement he made because I was saved before him and because of certain mistakes that he had made as a result of satanic attacks.

THANK GOD FOR HIS MERCIES AND DELIVERANCE

I was delivered by the Lord from my curse not too long ago in 2004. During my period of bondage, I was still receiving scriptures from God and was still very prayerful. I was still hearing from God, which made it difficult for me to repent because I thought that the fact that I was still hearing from

God meant that I had the right attitude. I thought if I was sinning, then the Lord would have stopped using me. I did not consider the many members we had lost or the dropping our tithes and offerings as a result of my behaviour. I decided to preach more "fire and brimstone" in order to lead people to Heaven.

Then, during the period of April 2003 to April 2004, I lost so much weight that I nearly died. I saw death! People began to get concerned because of my weight loss. A friend of mine, Pastor Mercy Ezekiel, saw me in January 2004 and advised me to take a break because I had young children and the pressure of the work of the ministry was affecting me. I took her advice to heart. It was the beginning stage of my deliverance.

Then I was finally fully delivered when I started studying Galatians 5:22-23.

Within one month of studying this scripture, the Lord asked me whether He could trust me enough to put people's lives into my hands. In answer to that question, I shouted, "But that is what you said in Matthew5:1!" I woke up by reading the scripture He had given in Matthew 5.

I received a different revelation to any that I had ever received before. I understood the true meaning of being the light and the salt of the earth. That is when my journey of deliverance started in earnest.

A week afterwards, Sky News showed on the television a man who was captured in Iraq. He was bound with chains from his hands to his feet. As I watched this news story, the Holy Spirit began to speak to me. He said, 'Do you know that anybody that goes to fight that man would be accused of being wicked, irrespective of the person's age, even if that person was a little child of five years old, because this man is helpless?'

The Holy Spirit continued to say, 'That is how it is in the realm of the spirit. Whoever fights those that are bound spiritually shall be accused of wickedness.' He went on to say that I must have compassion on the weak Christians and unbelievers alike. He said, 'If you do not have compassion on them you will be beaten in the spirit realm for beating someone who is bound with chains and fetters.'

PRAISE GOD FOR UNDERSTANDING

The above-mentioned course of events led to my deliverance. The Bible says "my people are destroyed from lack of knowledge" (Hosea 4:6). In all your getting, get knowledge and get understanding.

Praise God! I have minimised the level of my anger and

shouting. I am continually trying to portray the true image of Christ in all my actions. I have not arrived yet, but I try to forget the past and strive for the future.

The Devil tried to achieve a mass attack on my marriage in the church. He wanted me to be a bad example to the ladies in the church which could have resulted in strife and unhappiness for many. He wanted me to disobey the word of God by not behaving like a chosen vessel. The rate of divorce in all the churches is higher than outside of the churches, and the world's standard of doing things is being brought into the churches.

When I was living in disobedience I rejected every teaching about submission to husbands. I had a thousand and one excuses and reasons why my husband did not deserve my submission. My catchphrase was 'Respect is earned and not commanded.' I forgot that the Bible says that 'Only when my obedience is fulfilled can I avenge all disobedience.'

I took matters into my own hands instead of allowing God to fight my battles for me.

To the glory of God, today I am quick to apologise to anyone who feels offended by me. I could not do this during the period I was battling with self-righteousness. Jesus declared 'It is finished' on the cross.

CHAPTER 3: GENERATIONAL CURSES

Child of God, RELAX! It is well with you. Refuse self-condemnation and aspire to live a glorious life. Prayer changes things. I shall be praying for you. My prayer is that whosoever reads this book shall be delivered from every entanglement of the Devil.

CHAPTER 4

MORE ABOUT GENERATIONAL CURSES

God rewards the iniquities of the fathers unto the third and the fourth generations because of the influence of ancestral spirits which lead people to do what is not acceptable in the sight of God. The wrath of God comes upon the children of disobedience and the consequences of such disobedience are curses.

Even though God in his infinite mercy has provided a solution to the children of disobedient fathers, still the curses can be passed down from generation to generation because the environment a person is raised up in helps to structure that person.

The Bible tells us that the soul that sins shall die. Ezekiel 18:1-4:

> *^{1}The word of the LORD came to me: ^{2}"What do you people mean by quoting this proverb about the land of Israel: 'The parents eat sour grapes, and the children's teeth are set on edge'?*
> *^{3}"As surely as I live, declares the Sovereign LORD, you will no longer quote this proverb in Israel. ^{4}For everyone belongs to me, the parent as well as the child — both alike belong to me. The one who sins is the one who will die.*

Children act according to what they see adults do as they grow up. Parents may preach at their children to do what is right. Preaching is one thing, but acting it out is another! As children, we have to deliver ourselves through the constant studying of the Word of God. Study for yourself so that you will be able to live according to the Word of God. Do not study to be a judge because that will make you a hypocrite. Nobody is perfect. You have to show mercy and compassion on the sinner because you may not understand the influence of the Devil over him/her.

HOW TO APPLY SELF-DELIVERANCE

Acknowledge your faith before God and man. You must have a man or woman of God whom you can trust. You should go to such a fellow and share your problems with that person. Humble yourself and receive Godly counsel.

Consider James 5:13-20:

> [13]*Is anyone among you in trouble? Let them pray. Is anyone happy? Let them sing songs of praise.* [14]*Is anyone among you sick? Let them call the elders of the church to pray over them and anoint them with oil in the name of the Lord.* [15]*And the prayer offered in faith will make the sick person well; the Lord will raise them up. If they have sinned, they will be forgiven.* [16]*Therefore confess your sins to each other and pray for each other so that you may be healed. The prayer of a righteous person is powerful and effective.*
> [17]*Elijah was a human being, even as we are. He prayed earnestly that it would not rain, and it did not rain on the land for three and a half years.* [18]*Again he prayed, and the heavens gave rain, and the earth produced its crops.*
> [19]*My brothers and sisters, if one of you should wander from the truth and someone should bring that person back,* [20]*remember this: Whoever turns a sinner from the error of their ways will save them from death and cover over a multitude of sins.*

Who are the religious people? They are those who believe in the finished work of Calvary. They are those who trust and believe that God is the source of every good work and that God wants us to shine as lights. Righteousness is not by your own works and, therefore, your minister, this man or woman of God whom you trust, will not condemn you but will show you how to live a victorious life. You need to renounce every covenant you have knowingly or unknowingly entered into with the Devil; you need to cancel it out in the name of Jesus. If you have not confessed Jesus as your Saviour and Lord, tell the minister of God. The minister will reconcile you back to God through the powerful name of Jesus. If you do not know any servant of God who can help you, you can call our church office (the phone number is at the back of this book). We will help you into the glory of God. Once you have confessed Jesus Christ as your Lord and Redeemer, you will automatically become a righteous person in the sight of God. You cease to fight for yourself. Whatever touches you touches God. This scripture of Romans 5:1-21 will be a great help to you:

> [1]*Therefore, since we have been justified through faith, we have peace with God through our Lord Jesus Christ,* [2]*through whom we have gained access by faith into this grace in which we now stand. And we boast in the hope of the glory of God.* [3]*Not only so, but we also glory in our sufferings, because we know that suffering produces perseverance;* [4]*perseverance, character; and character,*

hope. *⁵And hope does not put us to shame, because God's love has been poured out into our hearts through the Holy Spirit, who has been given to us.*
⁶You see, at just the right time, when we were still powerless, Christ died for the ungodly. ⁷Very rarely will anyone die for a righteous person, though for a good person someone might possibly dare to die. ⁸But God demonstrates his own love for us in this: While we were still sinners, Christ died for us.
⁹Since we have now been justified by his blood, how much more shall we be saved from God's wrath through him! ¹⁰For if, while we were God's enemies, we were reconciled to him through the death of his Son, how much more, having been reconciled, shall we be saved through his life! ¹¹Not only is this so, but we also boast in God through our Lord Jesus Christ, through whom we have now received reconciliation.
¹²Therefore, just as sin entered the world through one man, and death through sin, and in this way death came to all people, because all sinned —
¹³To be sure, sin was in the world before the law was given, but sin is not charged against anyone's account where there is no law. ¹⁴Nevertheless, death reigned from the time of Adam to the time of Moses, even over those who did not sin by breaking a command, as did Adam, who is a pattern of the one to come.
¹⁵But the gift is not like the trespass. For if the many died by the trespass of the one man, how much more did God's

grace and the gift that came by the grace of the one man, Jesus Christ, overflow to the many! [16]*Nor can the gift of God be compared with the result of one man's sin: The judgment followed one sin and brought condemnation, but the gift followed many trespasses and brought justification.* [17]*For if, by the trespass of the one man, death reigned through that one man, how much more will those who receive God's abundant provision of grace and of the gift of righteousness reign in life through the one man, Jesus Christ!*
[18]*Consequently, just as one trespass resulted in condemnation for all people, so also one righteous act resulted in justification and life for all people.* [19]*For just as through the disobedience of the one man the many were made sinners, so also through the obedience of the one man the many will be made righteous.*
[20]*The law was brought in so that the trespass might increase. But where sin increased, grace increased all the more,* [21]*so that, just as sin reigned in death, so also grace might reign through righteousness to bring eternal life through Jesus Christ our Lord.*

Be equipped with the knowledge of who you are in Christ and how He sees you. Tear down the evil covenant your forefathers have built. You must uproot every tree your heavenly father has not planted (Jeremiah 1:10).

HOW DO YOU DO THIS?

It is very important that you understand how things work in the spirit realm. An arm of the flesh will definitely fail you. Some people travel to their own town, especially those from Africa, to destroy or burn down the shrines and temples their forefathers had built. You do not necessarily have to do that.

How did Jesus defeat the Devil? It was by the word of his mouth. Jesus quoted the written word to Satan in Luke 4:1-22:

> [1]*Jesus, full of the Holy Spirit, left the Jordan and was led by the Spirit into the wilderness,* [2]*where for forty days he was tempted by the Devil. He ate nothing during those days, and at the end of them he was hungry.*
> [3]*The Devil said to him, "If you are the Son of God, tell this stone to become bread."*
> [4]*Jesus answered, "It is written: 'Man shall not live on bread alone.'"*
> [5]*The Devil led him up to a high place and showed him in an instant all the kingdoms of the world.* [6]*And he said to him, "I will give you all their authority and splendour; it has been given to me, and I can give it to anyone I want to.* [7]*If you worship me, it will all be yours."*
> [8]*Jesus answered, "It is written: 'Worship the Lord your God and serve him only.'"*

⁹The Devil led him to Jerusalem and had him stand on the highest point of the temple. "If you are the Son of God," he said, "throw yourself down from here. ¹⁰For it is written: 'He will command his angels concerning you to guard you carefully; ¹¹they will lift you up in their hands, so that you will not strike your foot against a stone.'"

¹²Jesus answered, "It is said: 'Do not put the Lord your God to the test.'"

¹³When the Devil had finished all this tempting, he left him until an opportune time.

¹⁴Jesus returned to Galilee in the power of the Spirit, and news about him spread through the whole countryside. ¹⁵He was teaching in their synagogues, and everyone praised him. ¹⁶He went to Nazareth, where he had been brought up, and on the Sabbath day he went into the synagogue, as was his custom. He stood up to read, ¹⁷and the scroll of the prophet Isaiah was handed to him. Unrolling it, he found the place where it is written:

¹⁸"The Spirit of the Lord is on me, because he has anointed me to proclaim good news to the poor. He has sent me to proclaim freedom for the prisoners and recovery of sight for the blind, to set the oppressed free, ¹⁹to proclaim the year of the Lord's favour."

²⁰Then he rolled up the scroll, gave it back to the attendant and sat down. The eyes of everyone in the synagogue were fastened on him. ²¹He began by saying to them, "Today this scripture is fulfilled in your hearing."

²²All spoke well of him and were amazed at the gracious words that came from his lips. "Isn't this Joseph's son?" they asked.

If Jesus defeated Satan by using the word of God, so can you! You, too, have to defeat him by the written word you speak. Verses 8-12 of Jeremiah 1 say:

> Be not afraid of their faces. For I am with thee to deliver thee saith the Lord. ⁹Then the Lord put forth his hands and touched my mouth, and He said unto me ¹⁰behold have put my words in thy mouth. ¹¹Moreover the word of the Lord came unto me saying "Jeremiah what seeth thou" and I said I see a rod of an almond tree" Then said the Lord unto me, 'Thou has well seen: for I will hasten my word to perform it.'

When we confess Christ as our Saviour, we are in agreement with the word of God and that brings salvation.

Read Romans 10:8-10:

> *⁸ But what does it say? "The word is near you; it is in your mouth and in your heart"; that is, the message concerning faith that we proclaim: ⁹If you declare with your mouth, "Jesus is Lord," and believe in your heart that God raised him from the dead, you will be saved. ¹⁰For it is with your heart that you believe and are justified, and it is with your mouth that you profess your faith and are saved.*

Unless the Holy Spirit specifically tells you to go and tear down or destroy those shrines of your forefathers, my advice to you is *do not do it*. Do not fight against flesh and blood because the elders of your family will put a curse on you and you will create more enemies then friends. They will oppose you and refuse to be born again, no matter how you may witness to them about Jesus.

Read Ephesians 6:10-19:

> *[10]Finally, be strong in the Lord and in his mighty power. [11]Put on the full armor of God, so that you can take your stand against the Devil's schemes. [12]For our struggle is not against flesh and blood, but against the rulers, against the authorities, against the powers of this dark world and against the spiritual forces of evil in the heavenly realms. [13]Therefore put on the full armor of God, so that when the day of evil comes, you may be able to stand your ground, and after you have done everything, to stand. [14]Stand firm then, with the belt of truth buckled around your waist, with the breastplate of righteousness in place, [15]and with your feet fitted with the readiness that comes from the gospel of peace.*
> *[16]In addition to all this, take up the shield of faith, with which you can extinguish all the flaming arrows of the evil one. [17]Take the helmet of salvation and the sword of the Spirit, which is the word of God.*
> *[18]And pray in the Spirit on all occasions with all kinds of*

prayers and requests. With this in mind, be alert and always keep on praying for all the Lord's people. [19]Pray also for me, that whenever I speak, words may be given me so that I will fearlessly make known the mystery of the gospel...

Remember that in Matthew 17 Jesus sent Peter to go to the sea to get money in order for them to pay their taxes so they would not offend the tax collectors. You challenge the forces of darkness by your character and by refusing to behave the way of the world, and also by being a light in the midst of this crooked and wicked generation. And also by living according to the Word of God and bearing the Fruit of the Spirit, as mentioned in Galatians 5:22-23: "But the fruit of the Spirit is love, joy, peace, forbearance, kindness, goodness, faithfulness, gentleness and self-control. Against such things there is no law."

In 1996, I lost a relative of mine, my uncle, Vincent Ohalete. When I went to my town that same year, I was told that the host of my deceased uncle was harassing the people of my village. I was told that a witch doctor had already been consulted to come and deal with this menace. (Talk about the blind leading the blind!) The witch doctor, of course, could not do anything to help them, so they sent for another one. This time they wanted my uncle's body to be exhumed and burned; they did as the witch doctor said, but to no avail. Their torment continued and, when I heard this, I was grieved in my spirit and I sought for the cooperation of the local pastor to interpret the local dialect for the benefit of Vincent's wives and children. I explained to them that he was dead and, therefore, had no more authority over them. I told them that the living had no relationship with the dead. I also preached the message of salvation to them and they soon confessed that Christ was their Saviour and Lord. After their confession, we sang some praise songs in my local dialect (Igbo). The song went like this:

> There is power in Heaven
> There is power on Earth
> There is power everywhere
> But Jesus' power is supreme!

When we had finished singing this song, I rebuked the evil spirit that had been using Vincent to torment the people, and I bound him in the matchless name of Jesus. That was the end of the matter.

Now, Vincent had a son who refused to join us in the prayer of salvation, claiming that he was a Muslim. But, within a month this same man started going to church in Lagos, Nigeria. During his sleep one day he dreamt that his deceased father appeared to him and queried why he was sleeping on a particular bed (which apparently Vincent had bequeathed to another, more favoured son before his death). The sleeping son had no explanation, so his father's ghost slapped him in the dream.

When the son woke up the following morning, he had severe stomach cramps and pain. He told the dream to many people. The pain became so severe and sharp that he decided to go to the hospital. A doctor diagnosed the cause of the pain as appendicitis and demanded payment for treatment in advance before performing the operation. The young man went to his cousin to borrow the money but, as he and his cousin were on their way back to the hospital, he died. His cousin could not believe his eyes when cockroaches began to manifest from the dead body. The body was abandoned there and everyone around ran for their lives.

The Bible says evil will visit Jerusalem because they did not know the hour of visitation. The Bible encourages us to call on the name of the Lord while He is near, to seek him when he can be found (Isaiah 55:6).

In 1991, months after we started the Dynamic Gospel Church, a lady in her fifties came to us for help. According to her, she saw a ghost sitting on the stairs of the council house she had just moved into. She was frightened by the sight. In the morning when she told her neighbours of her encounter, they told her that the description she gave matched that of the former tenant who committed suicide in that flat. This lady lost her sleep because of what she heard and, therefore, resorted to drinking to dull her fear. Of course, this drinking could not help her.

When my husband and I went to pray for her, the Lord revealed to me where this lady was trying to fetch water with a basket. In that vision, she tried several times with this basket but because baskets are not watertight, she could not accomplish collecting any water. I shared the vision with her, but she pretended as though she did not understand me. The next morning when I woke up to pray and intercede in my usual manner, I felt the Lord reminding me of the vision and He told me to read Jeremiah 2:13, which states: "My people have committed two sins: they have forsaken me, the spring of living water, and have dug their own cisterns, broken cisterns that cannot hold water."

Praise the Lord, we serve a Mighty God! My husband and I went back to this lady's flat to share with her the Word I received. As soon as I started talking, she went to her bed and brought some cans of beer from under her pillow and said to me, 'Now take it. Take it and go.' She knew what the broken cistern was. We had no clue.

The word of God is like a hammer that breaks the rock. One would have expected her to repent and to receive deliverance from the curse that was following her. But she was not ready and no one can force anybody to receive Christ.

CHAPTER 4: MORE ABOUT GENERATIONAL CURSES

DELIVERANCE IS IN THE WORD

Jesus said to Peter, 'Upon this revealed knowledge, I will build my church and the gates of hell shall not prevail against it.' Matthew 16: 13-20 reads:

> [13]*When Jesus came to the region of Caesarea Philippi, he asked his disciples, "Who do people say the Son of Man is?"*
> [14]*They replied, "Some say John the Baptist; others say Elijah; and still others, Jeremiah or one of the prophets."*
> [15]*"But what about you?" he asked. "Who do you say I am?"*
> [16]*Simon Peter answered, "You are the Messiah, the Son of the living God."*
> [17]*Jesus replied, "Blessed are you, Simon son of Jonah, for this was not revealed to you by flesh and blood, but by my Father in heaven.* [18]*And I tell you that you are Peter, and on this rock I will build my church, and the gates of Hades will not overcome it.* [19]*I will give you the keys of the kingdom of heaven; whatever you bind on earth will be bound in heaven, and whatever you loose on earth will be loosed in heaven."* [20]*Then he ordered his disciples not to tell anyone that he was the Messiah.*

The key to the kingdom of Heaven is revelational knowledge. From the beginning of the world, God wanted his people to depend on him for guidance. He gave Adam and Eve power over everything he created but forbade them to eat of the Tree of Knowledge of good and evil. His intention is that we must trust in him to lead us in all things. Satan deceived Adam and Eve and they sinned against God. To be restored we must depend on God and the word of prophecy which he reveals from time to time. Jesus, the last Adam, came and restored us back to God. Our lives must be God made and not manmade. There are too many false prophets around these days, as Paul warned us in Acts 20:28-31:

> [28]*Keep watch over yourselves and all the flock of which the Holy Spirit has made you overseers. Be shepherds of the church of God, which he bought with his own blood.* [29]*I know that after I leave, savage wolves will come in among you and will not spare the flock.* [30]*Even from your own number men will arise and distort the truth in order to draw away disciples after them.* [31]*So be on your guard! Remember that for three years I never stopped warning each of you night and day with tears.*

Many Christians are gullible because they do not have the time to study the Word of life – the Bible - for themselves. They rely on what the preachers say from the pulpit.

CHAPTER 5

SOME SOLUTIONS IN DEALING WITH ANCESTRAL OR FAMILIAR SPIRITS

If you are born-again (by that, I mean you have confessed Jesus as your personal Saviour and Lord), you need to know your covenant rights.

Remember that you are in a covenant relationship with Christ.

A covenant is an agreement between two parties; there is a covenant between a believer and Jesus Christ. There is an emphasis placed on good work, noted in Ephesians 2:10: "For we are God's handiwork, created in Christ Jesus to do good works, which God prepared in advance for us to do."

God's promises are conditional. If you obey His commandments you will reap his blessings. For example, the righteous are to walk by faith in Jesus (Galatians 3:6-11).

So, also, Abraham "believed God, and it was credited to him as righteousness." Understand, then, that those who have faith are children of Abraham. Scripture foresaw that God would justify the Gentiles by faith, and announced the gospel in advance to Abraham: "All nations will be blessed through you." So those who rely on faith are blessed along with Abraham, the man of faith. For all who rely on the works of the law are under a curse, as it is written: "Cursed is everyone who does not continue to do everything written in the Book of the Law." Clearly no one who relies on the law is justified before God, because "the righteous will live by faith."

Tell the Devil you are a covenant child. You may have entered into a covenant with the Devil through past involvement but now you are a child of God, in a covenant relationship with Jesus. In the same way that it is wrong for you to bear your formal husband's name once you have divorced, and for a man to claim hold upon his ex-wife, it is wrong for you to enter into a covenant relationship with Jesus and yet portray the characteristics of the Devil (although we all know that that conversion is a gradual process). Likewise, it is wrong for the Devil to claim a born-again Christian. You cannot serve the Devil and Jesus at the same time! Light and darkness have nothing in common; nor can you serve two masters at a time. Decide to fight the battle in your heart and mind today.

Act like a child of God. It may not be easy. You may even think it is not working, but be encouraged that it is. Submit yourself to God and continue to resist the Devil and his negative thoughts and he will flee from you. (James 4:7)

Start to live what is good and abhor evil. Forgive those that have caused you any hurt. Remember that vengeance is the Lord's. Forget your past; focus on your future. Decide to make a difference. Remember those who have been trapped by the Devil as they will look to you for encouragement as they believe God and turn over on to a clean and new page of their life.

Try not to repeat the mistakes that your parents and family made!

FORGIVE AND FORGET

This is a very important step towards your deliverance. Remember the Mark 11:24-26 scripture discussed earlier in this book.

There is a mass exodus from many churches and spiritual prostitution because of the spirit of offence. The pastor or the elders may have offended you but, remember, they are also human beings like you. Nobody is perfect. We are running the race. Your husband or wife may have let you down; that should not have to result in a divorce. Jesus said, "When I return, shall I find faith?" Faith is believing that all shall be well.

Since Jesus has defeated Satan on your behalf all you need is constant prayer coupled with endurance while you look unto JESUS, the Author and Finisher of your Faith. (Read the parable of the persistent widow in Luke 18.)

Having said this, please—run for your life if staying in that marriage will cost you your life! It is better to separate and live than to remain and die.

There appear to be more breakaways in spirit-filled Christians than with other empty religions. Why? It has to do with the spirit of offence. The irony is that innocent members and their families are caught up in the fighting within the body of Christ.

Pastors may boast about having the largest and fastest growing churches at the expense of other pastors whose churches they have emptied in order to fill the empty seats in their own church.

Brethren, is this of Christ? Does the living Bible teach us to do this? Jesus is coming very soon. Let us repent of certain practices which are anti-Christian.

Many pastors call themselves into full-time ministries. They have ordained themselves bishops, apostles, prophets, and prophetesses without holding any of the qualifications listed in 1Timothy 3:1-15.

> [1]*Here is a trustworthy saying: Whoever aspires to be an overseer desires a noble task.*
> [2]*Now the overseer is to be above reproach, faithful to his wife, temperate, self-controlled, respectable, hospitable, able to teach,* [3]*not given to drunkenness, not violent but gentle, not quarrelsome, not a lover of money.*
> [4]*He must manage his own family well and see that his children obey him, and he must do so in a manner worthy of full respect.* [5]*(If anyone does not know how to manage his own family how can he take care of God's church?)*
> [6]*He must not be a recent convert, or he may become conceited and fall under the same judgment as the Devil.*

⁷He must also have a good reputation with outsiders, so that he will not fall into disgrace and into the Devil's trap. ⁸In the same way, deacons are to be worthy of respect, sincere, not indulging in much wine, and not pursuing dishonest gain. ⁹They must keep hold of the deep truths of the faith with a clear conscience.
¹⁰They must first be tested; and then if there is nothing against them, let them serve as deacons. ¹¹In the same way, the women are to be worthy of respect, not malicious talkers but temperate and trustworthy in everything.
¹²A deacon must be faithful to his wife and must manage his children and his household well. ¹³Those who have served well gain an excellent standing and great assurance in their faith in Christ Jesus.
¹⁴Although I hope to come to you soon, I am writing you these instructions so that, ¹⁵if I am delayed, you will know how people ought to conduct themselves in God's household, which is the church of the living God, the pillar and foundation of the truth.

Many ministers and deacons have no spiritual patents, and have received no godly counsel. They are not responsible to anybody, neither do they respect anybody. I am not judging or condemning anyone; I am only exposing the activities of ancestral and familial spirits and generational curses. These spirits are responsible for the ungodly and unchristian attitudes and characters that are being manifested in our churches these days. I ask that you be sure of yourself before praying for these ministers by the laying on of hands (1Timothy 5:22).

You must understand why these ancestral spirits want to influence you. Their assignment is to make you disobey God through negative things you do or say that are against the word of God. Therefore, guard your heart and mind with the Sword of the Spirit. Refuse to think or say what the enemy of your soul wants you to think or say. Study the word of God to know the role God wants you to play. Carry out your own God-given assignment and leave other people to God. He will deal with their character flaws and weaknesses. But the Devil will want to remind you of the bad things that were done against you to provoke you to revenge. God says "Vengeance is mine." You cannot avenge any disobedience until your own obedience is fulfilled, which means your prayers or intercessions for anybody else will not bear fruit until you have obeyed God in that area, too. No wonder some of us intercessors pray night and day without much evidence!

The result of disobedience is upsetting God and, thereby, the hindering your blessings. Demonic spirits remind you of all the evil things people have said or done against you just to upset you or instigate you to murmur against them.

No matter what the reason for your murmuring, murmuring is against the will of God. God hates that. When you murmur against a child of God, you deny all the good things God has used the person to do for you. In other words, you murmur against the Lord as well! When the children of Israel murmured against Moses, God become angry with them. Read for yourself the account of what happened to them in Numbers 21.

Child of God, decide to serve God with thanksgiving in your heart (Philippians 4:6). Romans 8:28 says that all things work for good to those who love God. Christianity is a relationship that must be nurtured with thanksgiving.

DETERMINATION IS THE KEY

Ancestral spirits affect people from generation to generation. The negative effect is called a 'generational curse'. A generational curse will hold its grip on an individual irrespective of the where that person lives or where they were born.

When I was in America in 1993, I met a black pastor whose character was very similar to that of African men who live in Nigeria. During our discussion, his wife exclaimed, "My husband's lineage must be Nigerian," and the pastor said, "I have always had an inclination in my spirit that I am connected to Nigeria."

CHAPTER 5: SOME SOLUTIONS IN DEALING WITH ANCESTRAL OR FAMILIAR SPIRITS

Most times, people blame slave masters for their predicament. They blame their teachers for their failure to pass examinations. They blame their parents for inadequate care. They blame the Government for relegating them to the slums and ghetto areas.

The blame game is another subtle method the Devil uses to keep people bound. So long as there is someone to blame for your failures, you will never get up to fight these ancestral spirits that work to keep you bound.

I read one of Chinua Achebe's books in which he wrote how his father died when he was a child. During his secondary school education, most of the other students' parents visited them in cars and brought lots of goodies. He was always waiting for his poor mother to walk from her village to his school with one or two items for him. She had always visited with one coconut. Mr. Achebe said that he had determined in his mind that, while these other students may have had more worldly goods than him, he would beat them both in academics and in athletics. His determination bore fruit: he became one of the best writers Africa has ever produced. He chose to make a difference and that made all the difference.

IT'S ALL ABOUT CHOICE

I heard a true story of a set of twins whose father was drunkard. One of the boys became a drunkard like their father, while the other one studied, worked hard, and became a very successful man. Both of them were interviewed separately. The one that was drinking said that because his father was a drunkard he had no choice but to be like his father. The successful twin disassociated himself from the behaviour of his father and his twin brother. He purposed in his heart not to be like them. He worked hard to make a difference.

Whatever decisions you make today will affect your tomorrow. The difference between a road sweeper and a medical doctor is the decision they made during their primary and secondary school years.

It is not too late; you can make a U-turn. You can turn a new page. Today, if you hear His voice, do not harden your heart. Confess your sins to God, in the name of Jesus Christ our Lord and Saviour. Repent of your sins and your weaknesses. Ask God to help you; He is the only one that has the power to change your circumstances. If you are not well-educated, there are many universities that offer part-time classes all over the world, even in African countries. Get registered to study in any area of your choice.

CHAPTER 5: SOME SOLUTIONS IN DEALING WITH ANCESTRAL OR FAMILIAR SPIRITS

Stop deceiving yourself by using big/false titles. No matter how big your title, you will still feel a vacuum whenever you are in the mist of educated people until you have educated yourself. It is amazing how young pastors who do not even have a building of their own, no branches, no substantial evidence of pastoring, are now bearing such titles as 'Bishop', 'Reverend', 'Doctor', and so on, just to boost their egos.

My beloved brethren, you need to reconsider your actions, whether they are based on pride or achievement. When you look into the lie of the Devil, the one who ordained these individuals, you will find it is all a gimmick.

The world is watching us, the born-again children of God. Big titles are commonly found among black Christian leaders. Again, I consider the use of big/false titles to be one of the methods ancestral spirits use to bring down a humble character, and our character should be reflected in our relationship with God and with our fellow human beings.

CHAPTER 6

HOW TO DEAL WITH THE CONFUSION CAUSED BY ANCESTRAL AND FAMILIAR SPIRITS

Once I travelled on a mission with a self-declared prophetess. This lady abandoned her husband and children when she was born-again and fled to England. She joined a church in England and told me that the Holy Spirit had asked her to start a fellowship there. She started this fellowship in her flat without the knowledge of her senior pastor. Her flat mate, who attended the same church as she, went and informed their pastor of the fellowship on her behalf. The senior pastor then invited her to come and discuss the fellowship with him. She declined the invitation.

One week later, she made an appointment to see her senior pastor. He refused to see her. She then took offence, saying that the pastor had disobeyed the Holy Spirit. I corrected her, telling her that the Holy Spirit is not an author of confusion, and then gave her the following scriptures to read: Timothy 6:1-5, Romans 13:1-8, 2 Peter1:1-12, and 2 Peter 2:1-11.

This lady is younger than I both in age and in her ministry. She scolded me for correcting her and told me that she was not obligated to answer to anyone; she openly admitted that she had no mentors and no friends in the ministry and that she did not need any.

One day she said God told her to borrow money to pay for the rent where she held her fellowship. Thereafter, they lost the flat because the people she approached to borrow money from refused to lend her anything. She said they had rebelled against the Holy Spirit. I was one of those people she approached. She wanted me to lend her £3,000 (three thousand pounds sterling). I did not have any conviction in my spirit to lend her the money and refused.

One month later, we went to a church meeting together. The young pastor of the church had a problem with accommodations regarding their place of worship. The Holy Spirit told me that my church should donate five thousand pounds (£5,000) towards the young man's church building, so we did. Later, when I asked this prophetess why God did not approve her open request of my lending her money, but had given me encouragement to donate to this other fellow who had not even made a request, she flew into a rage and began to abuse me. Today, she has cards which she distributes which describe her as prophetess or senior pastor of her ministry.

This is evidence of the work of familiar spirit. I have not written this to criticize this dear sister, but to highlight how the Devil can make some people very stubborn and non-repentant. She has struggled in her ministry for ten years without much success.

Take special consideration of this story if you are a self-made minister who does not respect anybody or want to relate with anybody except the Holy Spirit. Please note that everybody needs help. Jesus Christ could have done everything himself yet he had a group of people whom He called Disciples to work with Him. He allowed John the Baptist to baptise him to fulfil all righteousness.

We need one another. We must serve one another. Elisha

died with his anointing because of the bad attitude of Gehazi, a bad attitude which was caused by a familiar spirit.

TERRITORIAL SPIRITS

These are the evil spirits which want to control and influence the activities of people that live in a particular locality. For example, in London, England, the character of the youngsters who live in Brixton, Stockwell, and Oval are quite different from those of the young people who live in Golders Green on the other side of London. This difference in character can be observed from one place to another, from one country to another, all around the world.

A good example of the activities of these territorial spirits can be found in Daniel 10:1-14:

> *In the third year of Cyrus king of Persia, a revelation was given to Daniel (who was called Belteshazzar). Its message was true and it concerned a great war. The understanding of the message came to him in a vision.*
> *²At that time I, Daniel, mourned for three weeks. ³I ate no choice food; no meat or wine touched my lips; and I used no lotions at all until the three weeks were over.*
> *⁴On the twenty-fourth day of the first month, as I was standing on the bank of the great river, the Tigris, ⁵I looked up and there before me was a man dressed in linen, with*

CHAPTER 6: HOW TO DEAL WITH THE CONFUSION CAUSED BY ANCESTRAL AND FAMILIAR SPIRITS

a belt of fine gold from Uphaz around his waist. ⁶His body was like topaz, his face like lightning, his eyes like flaming torches, his arms and legs like the gleam of burnished bronze, and his voice like the sound of a multitude.
⁷I, Daniel, was the only one who saw the vision; those who were with me did not see it, but such terror overwhelmed them that they fled and hid themselves. ⁸So I was left alone, gazing at this great vision; I had no strength left, my face turned deathly pale and I was helpless. ⁹Then I heard him speaking, and as I listened to him, I fell into a deep sleep, my face to the ground.
¹⁰A hand touched me and set me trembling on my hands and knees. ¹¹He said, "Daniel, you who are highly esteemed, consider carefully the words I am about to speak to you, and stand up, for I have now been sent to you." And when he said this to me, I stood up trembling.
¹²Then he continued, "Do not be afraid, Daniel. Since the first day that you set your mind to gain understanding and to humble yourself before your God, your words were heard, and I have come in response to them. ¹³But the prince of the Persian kingdom resisted me twenty-one days. Then Michael, one of the chief princes, came to help me, because I was detained there with the king of Persia. ¹⁴Now I have come to explain to you what will happen to your people in the future, for the vision concerns a time yet to come."

The only remedy able to counter the negative influences of these spirits is to pray with and for your children every morning. You must make time to pray with them before they go to school. Cover them with the blood of Jesus. Cancel and nullify every negative influence. Refuse any negative transfer of spirits that would want to hide in your children because of their association with strange children at school. Prayer changes things.

My son went to a birthday party when he was three years old. A pastor's daughter was celebrating her birthday (This pastor's wife had a water spirit husband. This is the same lady that the Lord showed to me when he appeared to me and I asked him to give me the spirit of discernment. The Lord answered by revealing this beautiful lady to me, when suddenly before my very eyes her image changed to that of a masquerade with fierce teeth and bulging eyes. When I shared this revelation with her husband, a pastor of a church that had come to England to pursue a Doctorate degree program, he admitted that his wife had spiritual problems associated with the water; spiritual problems are normally referred to as 'spirit husbands'.)

I was at home praying when my son returned from that birthday party. Immediately he came in, I saw another young boy that had the same features as my son walk in with him. I prayerfully asked the Lord to reveal my real son to me to enable me to cast away the false one. I took authority over the false one and cast him out. This is what is called 'transference of spirit'. If I had not cast it out, it would have grown with my son. This false spirit would have influenced my son's character without my knowledge. I may have hit my son, scolded him, or even taken him to a psychologist, but the real cause of the problem would have been spiritual rather than physical.

We are living in perilous times, so — please, parents! — take extra time in prayer to intercede for your children. It is good to give them a good education and a quality life style, but the most important thing is to teach them a God-fearing life that will make them good citizens and lead them to eternal life. The Devil and his demons have plans to influence people's lives to do evil, thereby causing them to disobey God and go to Hell, BUT YOU NEED TO PRAY AND CANCEL EVERY EVIL PLAN OF THE ENEMY against you and your family in Jesus' name.

If you notice any form of immorality or unstable characteristics in your child, go to your pastor (if you have one) or write to me at the address at the back of this book. I shall go with you in prayer to cast out the unclean spirit in Jesus' name. Shame is not your portion. Jesus died for you and has given you victory over every work of the enemy. Be careful and prayerfully choose your friends. Also, try and monitor the behaviour and characteristics of your children and their friends. There are some friends you need to pray out of your child's life. You should not try to place an embargo on your children's friends because it may cause resentment. However, remember that the prayer of a righteous man/woman avails much.

WHO IS A RIGHTEOUS PERSON?

A righteous person is somebody who's plan and will is to obey every word that proceeds out of the mouth of God. That is obedience to the word of God. A righteous person's will is that the perfect will of God be done, not only in their life, but on the whole earth. A righteous person has sold their entire life to God. They do not do anything to please the flesh but do all things to please God.

The Bible describes the characteristic of a righteous man in Romans 2:13-16:

> *For it is not those who hear the law who are righteous in God's sight, but it is those who obey the law who will be declared righteous. ¹⁴(Indeed, when Gentiles, who do not have the law, do by nature things required by the law, they are a law for themselves, even though they do not have the law. ¹⁵They show that the requirements of the law are written on their hearts, their consciences also bearing witness, and their thoughts sometimes accusing them and at other times even defending them.) ¹⁶This will take place*

on the day when God judges people's secrets through Jesus Christ, as my gospel declares.

When Elijah prayed that they should be no rain for 3½ years, he did not pray because he wanted to exhibit his powers but because he was vexed by the level of disobedience and immorality going on in Israel. God answered Elijah's prayers because he was on God's side. Remember again: God is no respecter of persons! Likewise, God spared Noah from the flood because of his righteousness.

Jesus came to earth and redeemed us from all unrighteousness. Therefore, we became the righteousness of God in Christ Jesus. Does your life show any signs of redemption? Does your life glorify God or does it make people blaspheme His holy name? Who is in control of your life? Do you use the grace of God to allow the Devil to control your life? Please, try and make an effort to allow your life to reflect the power of the finished work of Calvary! If you are struggling, go to a true man or woman of God for deliverance. I am not talking about the ten and 21 days deliverance that we often hear about. I am talking about the type of deliverance Jesus did, and which Paul and his team did in Acts 16. The Word tells us that the Devil left that same hour. Be careful who you allow to lay hands on you! Test every spirit. This is very important because, according to Matthew 7:21-23, not everybody that heals and performs miracles in the name of Jesus is genuine. Nobody is perfect but there are truly some who are wolves in sheep's skin.

According to Philippians 3, some individuals come into the ministry for their bellies. God recently gave me an illustration about people who sin with the confidence that God's grace will cover them. God told me to consider how many Christians are suffering to see his glory manifested in their lives. They do not see the purpose of their obedience, and wrongly believe that grace will cover them. The situation is made worse by false Christians who influence them and encourage them to sin. It is like fuel or kerosene which is added to the water which has been collected and preserved in a reservoir. This water can be easily contaminated or polluted! These false brethren refuse to understand that some Christians have suffered for the gospel.

After giving me this illustration, God then asked me, 'How can I continue to allow these false brethren to persist in polluting the water at the expense of many Christians who have laboured in the gospel to bring light to the world?'

Brethren, let us Endeavour to fight the good fight of faith. Faith is a fighter. You have to fight for the promise of God upon your life. The kingdom of God suffers violence and the violent ones aspire to take the Kingdom by force.

CHAPTER 7

DREAMS AND VISIONS

Man is a spirit that lives in a physical human body. The real man is not the physical body that one can see with the naked eye. The real man is hidden inside the body. God is a spirit and He created us as spirits, but He provided a temporary shelter for that spirit which consists of the body that we see. Consider 2Corinthians 5:1-6:

> For we know that if the earthly tent we live in is destroyed, we have a building from God, an eternal house in heaven, not built by human hands. ²Meanwhile we groan, longing to be clothed instead with our heavenly dwelling, ³because when we are clothed, we will not be found naked. ⁴For while we are in this tent, we groan and are burdened,

> *because we do not wish to be unclothed but to be clothed instead with our heavenly dwelling, so that what is mortal may be swallowed up by life. [5]Now the one who has fashioned us for this very purpose is God, who has given us the Spirit as a deposit, guaranteeing what is to come. [6]Therefore we are always confident and know that as long as we are at home in the body we are away from the Lord.*

There are two spirits ruling this world: the spirit of God, which is the supreme spirit, and the spirit of the Devil. Man's spirit is weaker than these two spirits that rule the world. Thus, man's spirit must be ruled by one of the two stronger spirits. Both Heaven and Earth are controlled and ruled by spirits. Therefore, before anything happens in the physical it has to first of all happen in the spiritual world; whatever happens here in the visible world has already happened in the invisible world. Man can only communicate with the ruling spirit (whether it is the spirit of God or the spirit of the Devil) via his own spirit. John 4:24 reads: "God is spirit, and his worshipers must worship in the Spirit and in truth."

The two most common ways for man to communicate with the ruling spirits are through dreams and visions. Other methods include prayers to God the Father in the name of Jesus, or prayers directly to idolatrous gods. As Christians mature in the things of God they will begin to communicate through the word of God which is the TRUTH.

There are Seven Spirits ruling on earth:

God Almighty; Jesus; the Holy Spirit; angelic spirits; the Devil; demonic spirits; and, finally, human beings.

God Almighty uses Jesus, the Holy Spirit, and angelic spirits that are obedient to Him to influence the human spirits to act as "light and salt" on earth. Human beings behave according to the spirit controlling them at any particular time.

The Devil uses satanic spirits which sometimes act as angels of light to deceive human beings to act in deceit towards other human beings. Satan has a hierarchy of Spirits he uses to act on his behalf.

All these Spirits fight to win control over human spirits. Man is the most important species on earth. Everything is centred on man. God created everything before He created man and gave man power and authority to rule the whole earth.

AUTHORITY IS HANDED OVER BY A SUPERIOR SPIRIT

The person to whom authority is handed over to can inevitably act on behalf of the higher being and his authority has the same effect as the higher person. It is like giving someone irrevocable power of attorney. This is why Satan uses men to act in a demonic and bad manner. Jesus gave back to man the authority and power he snatched from Satan (Luke 10:19).

SATANIC OPERATION

Satan is not omnipresent. He uses his demonic agents to operate. And he operates through human beings. There is a common saying: "It is Satan" or "It is the work of Satan". But does Satan use a person? Truly, the person who allows Satan to use him/her is the "Satan" I see. And I cannot be ignorant of the devices of Satan. Therefore, if I try to help anyone recognise the activities of Satan to no avail, my next course of action would be to distance myself from that person before I die an untimely death. I will not go to hell for acting wisely!

UNDERSTANDING AUTHORITY

Anyone who understands the authority and power in the name of Jesus can still perform miracle, signs and wonders even if this person's character does not glorify Jesus. WHY? There is power in the name and blood of Jesus. Mathew 7:21-23.

BE VIGILANT

Do not fall prey to wicked people who want to oppress you in the name of a leader of having authority over you. There is time for everything. Ecclesiastes 3:1-8. There is a time to rebuke and challenge hypocrites. Be wise as serpent and harmless as a dove.

DREAMS

The simplest way for a man to communicate with the spirit world is through dreams. Dreams can be either positive or negative and they can come from either God or the Devil. One cannot really judge the accuracy of a dream from its context. A positive dream can either come from God or Satan. For example, the Devil can lure a person into lust by showing them a luxurious car when that person doesn't have a corresponding source of income to enable them to purchase the car. Many Christians have erred because of some unbalanced prosperity messages they have had reinforced by dreams.

Let's look at 1Timothy 6:6-19. Verses 6-7 say: "But godliness with contentment is great gain. For we brought nothing into the world, and we can take nothing out of it." Anybody can dream irrespective of age. In Genesis 37, Joseph dreamed as a young man and his dreams came to pass.

Dreams are one of the ways our human spirits can communicate with the spirit world. Dreams can foretell the future or reflect things that have been happening around us which we were not aware of. Lives can be transformed by our dreams if we take the time to find out what they mean.

Dreams should be taken seriously no matter how void of truth they may seem. God used me and my husband to deliver a lady taunted by a devilish spirit. She used to wear underpants to bed and would dream that she lost these underpants in real life. She would wake up without them on. To prove that she not hallucinating, she would let her flat mates see her before she went to bed and upon waking she would again find that she was no longer wearing them and that they had been thrown to the other side of the room. This frustration continued for years.

When she came to London she thought that she had escaped the demons that used to steal her underwear, but alas the unusual events continued. When the lady involved brought these events to our attention we went to her flat and prayed, and God delivered her from the power of darkness.

Recently, we heard of a case in which a lady dreamt that she was shot and the bullets travelled through her neck to other parts of her body. She woke up to find that worm-like creatures were creeping around her neck and on the rest of her body. She still suffers from this strange attack. She has undergone almost every type of medical treatment, but all her treatments have been in vain.

I know another lady who failed her professional examination for many years and whatever she touched in those years was unsuccessful. This demon of failure followed her for over 12 years.

One day in 1987, after I had an encounter with the Lord Jesus, I began to inquire from the Lord the cause of this lady's failures. He revealed to me where she was bitten by a dog. I called this lady and shared the vision with her. She told me that she had had a dream many years ago when she travelled to her hometown in Africa that she had been bitten by a dog. She thought that this was ordinary dream; in truth, her future success had been tampered with in that dream. The dream she had was the source of her failures. To the glory of God, I took the matter up in prayer and the Lord told me that this lady had already failed her exams for that year but that in subsequent years she would be successful. The Lord went further to reveal the details of the examination pass marks with reference to one or two subjects, and what the Lord revealed is exactly what happened.

As I continued to seek the face of the Lord concerning this lady, the Lord Jesus through the Holy Spirit revealed to me in a dream the man that she would marry, describing his height and colour. I saw the man sweeping her flat with a long brush and, later in the dream, she appeared wearing a white dress with white sandals. In the dream she told me that she had been asked to go and see the Prime Minister. Immediately upon waking, I shared this dream with my husband, Joseph, and that this lady would soon be granted permanent residence in the United Kingdom. Within two months of this dream, the woman received her indefinite leave to remain in the UK after having fought a long battle with authorities concerning her stay.

Three years later, the same lady got married to a friend of ours. The man had been revealed to me in a dream sweeping; in reality he is a minister of the gospel, which relates to spiritual cleansing. Amazingly, when God revealed these things we knew nothing either about this man or his intentions to marry this lady. In fact, the man was still in Africa when God revealed his plan and purpose regarding the marriage relationship.

The key point to remember about this story is that God has given us power to trade on serpents and scorpions and over all the powers of the enemy and that nothing shall, by any means, hurt us (Luke 10:19).

Some may say that they do not believe in dreams or the Devil and that it is all superstition. I can tell you they are not. God is a real and Satan is just as real.

Before the Lord intervened on my behalf in 1988, I used to dream about my menstruation. I even decided not to record the dates because I would dream about menstruating in my dream so often. Each time I menstruated in the dream I would wake up bleeding my flow.

One night, after having the same dream, the Lord spoke to my heart and asked me to reject the dream and told me that they were not from Him. He went on to say that these dreams were the cause of my inability to conceive. I had waited for three and a half years to have another baby after our first son was born in March 1984, but it hadn't yet happened.

From that night on, every time I would have that dream I would reject it and cancel it immediately upon waking. The dreams continued coming until the ninth month of my pregnancy with my second child. The Lord told me that if I ever agreed with that dream I would lose my baby. The Bible says in Matthew 11:12: "And from the day of John the Baptist until now the Kingdom of Heaven suffereth violence and the violent take it by force."

The Lord had shown me the sex of my baby months before I conceived. I knew that I was about to receive what I had been praying and believing God for; I knew I could not allow the Devil to either exchange the baby or take her away. On a few occasions in the dream the Devil, through his agents that looked like friends of mine, had brought a baby boy to hand over to me. By God's grace I managed to reject their boy in the dream when it was offered because I knew it wasn't truth.

You see, the Devil can exchange the baby in the womb through dreams. The Lord permitted me to see in the spirit how such an exchange take place. Women who are having problems with conception sometimes go to witchdoctors or places where spiritual incantations are made. Sometimes, they will even perform child sacrifices—kidnapping children and killing them as a sacrifice to carry out rituals to appease the Devil. The Devil will implant the dead children in the womb of the woman concerned. He does this because he cannot create life and, therefore, he can only offer what is not his. To use a common phrase: "He will rob Peter to pay Paul"

Alternatively, as in my case, the Devil will exchange babies in a person's dream. A lady we know always lost her pregnancies through dreams. Each time she became pregnant, a demonic woman would appear in her dream. The demon would either rub its hand over her stomach or literally carry a baby away. Soon after the visitation, the lady would wake up and notice blood stains on her bed sheet. That would mark the end of the pregnancy and result in another miscarriage.

CHAPTER 7: DREAMS AND VISIONS

The Devil robs people of many blessings through dreams. Some people dream about going back to school to take examinations. In their dreams they will either not be able to complete the examination or the pen will not write or they would go to the examination hall without a pen. Such dreams entail a life of failure and deficiency.

In some dreams, a person will be waiting for a means of transport, either a bus or a train. Upon the arrival of the awaited transport the person would then miss the bus or train. This type of dream signifies set-backs of one type or another.

Whenever a person has this type of dream they should cancel it and reject it by standing upon the word of God, and in particular repeat and remember promises that relate to blessings and successes. Serious prayers need to be said and spiritual warfare should be entered into. This type of matter cannot be overcome with the usual five minute prayer of 'I thank you God; I reject this dream in Jesus name.' No! This type of curse is not overcome except by prayer and fasting! Your prayer should be backed up with fasting and should be the continuous, effective, fervent prayer of the righteous that avails much. Remind yourself always of what the Lord Jesus has done to redeem you from every curse of ill luck and remember that, when you were raised with Him through faith in the power of God, the ordinances that were held against you were cancelled.

Colossians 2:12-15 reads:

> ...*having been buried with him in baptism, in which you were also raised with him through your faith in the working of God, who raised him from the dead.*
> *¹³When you were dead in your sins and in the uncircumcision of your flesh, God made you alive with Christ. He forgave us all our sins, ¹⁴having cancelled the charge of our legal indebtedness, which stood against us and condemned us; he has taken it away, nailing it to the cross. ¹⁵And having disarmed the powers and authorities, he made a public spectacle of them, triumphing over them by the cross.*

See for yourself what Galatians 3:13-14 says about the born-again believer being redeemed from the curse of the law. Setback is not your portion!

Most negative dreams and mishaps are a result of past involvement with the satanic world. That involvement could have been through palm reading; a visit to a witchdoctor; reading of horoscopes; contact with demonic agents; sexual immorality; illegal dealings; worldly music such as punk rock; television soap operas; pornographic films and magazines; idol worship; sacrifice to idols in water, in the street, or in the bush; or any exchange of goods with the demonic spirit realm, including things like the pouring of libations during celebrations.

Blood covenants entered into ignorantly will also cause negative dreams and setbacks. Any blood covenant made with the Devil has to be broken. When people ignorantly have their bodies cut, the blood is used in a covenant with the Devil. The Devil performs this part of the covenant in heavenly places by attacking the unwitting partakers of the covenant.

As Christians, our only sacrifice should be in the form of worship to God the Almighty through Jesus Christ, our sacrificial lamb and redeemer. Only the name of Jesus and His precious blood can redeem us and cancel this agreement. Read on your own what Ephesians 1:20-23 says about the position of Jesus, our glorious Saviour, and remember that we, too, are "…[20]seated with Him at the right hand of God in heavenly places, [21]far above all principality, and power and might and dominion, and every name that is named, not only in this age but also in that which is to come."

The human spirit is weaker than the spirit of the Devil. When Adam rebelled against God, he gave over his spiritual authority to Satan (remember that the spiritual rules the physical). However, when an individual is born-again the spirit of God (which is stronger than the human spirit) steps in to cover our human spirit.

There is a case where a step-mother became angry with her

partner's children and she took her step-children's names to a witchdoctor and instructed him to ensure that the children would never amount to anything in life. This witchdoctor would call out the names of these children via a Mirror of Divination.

One of the children was born-again, and when the witchdoctor called on the child's name, the child's image would not appear in his mirror. The witchdoctor asked the woman to identify the young man by asking his name, his place of residence, and to what society he belonged because the witchdoctor could not make him appear in his mirror. The step-mother then told him that the young man belonged to a group sect called the Born-Again Movement and that he would go about with his Bible to prayer meetings, and that she did not know what they did there. The witch doctor told the lady to forget about the young man, that he could not harm him because he belonged to a stronger power. I say Amen to that!

The next person in the list was the young man's sister who was not born-again. Immediately when her name was called the girl's image emerged from the Mirror. This wicked man took a chain and carried out some incantation; he chained her image and locked the chain with a key. When the step-mother got home she told her step-daughter she would never get married. The young lady thought it was an idle threat.

Sometime in 1991, the Lord revealed the step-daughter to me. He told me where she was bound with a chain that was padlocked. When she came to see me she confessed that a group of spiritualists wearing white garments had revealed her bondage to her previously. They told her to buy certain items and took her to a cement artefact where they offered these things to the dead spirits. She agreed and did as she was told, thinking that the witchdoctor's word had been cancelled by these people. However, these are all agents of Satan. How can a demon undo what another demon has done? Rather, the problem will be compounded.

Matthew 12:25 reads: "Jesus knew their thoughts and said to them, 'Every kingdom divided against itself will be ruined, and every city or household divided against itself will not stand.'"

Because of what the witchdoctor had done the young lady had not been able to get married. Men would have loved to marry her, and some tried, but whenever they got close to the time of the wedding the men would always call the wedding off. We arranged a deliverance prayer for her but the demon would not allow her to come forth to us for its deliverance; she would give us one reason or another why it was not possible for her to attend the deliverance meeting. We knew that one day God would make it possible for her to be delivered. However, she ended up moving to another church where the pastor does not have the gift of discernment.

Zachariah 4:6 reads: "So he said to me, 'This is the word of the Lord to Zerubbabel: 'Not by might nor by power, but by my Spirit,' says the Lord Almighty.'"

Another lady approached me with a problem that she was experiencing in her marriage. She was told me that she had a water spirit oppressing her. She had married without going through a deliverance to deal with this water spirit husband. Before she married her physical husband she had already been married in the spirit world to a water spirit husband; her marriage to her physical husband did not nullify her first marriage to the evil spirit because the spiritual rules the physical. So, even in her husband's house, this evil spirit would visit her dreams. He would have intercourse with her and sometimes left her screaming for more; her screaming had woken her natural husband on several occasions.

Throughout the period prior to her deliverance, this woman would only enjoy sex with her spiritual husband. Whenever her physical husband approached her for sex she would refuse. This caused hatred and anger to develop in the marriage relationship. If she tried to allow him to make love to her out of sympathy, she would incur injuries on her private parts! She would lay like a log of wood, praying for him to get off her. This continued until she was prayerfully delivered. The water spirit almost killed her husband; the physical husband's future success was blocked. The man was rich before he married her, but, after his marriage, his wealth dried up. Although both the man and the woman were Christians before they got married, their Christianity did not prevent the evil water spirit husband from visiting the lady.

Claiming Christianity without both knowledge of the word of God and intensive prayer, makes one a weak Christian. The Devil does not concern himself with weak Christians. It does not matter to him how many times a person goes to church. What matters is how much of the living truth and authority God has given us and whether we are able to use that power effectively.

Anybody who disobeys police has implicitly disobeyed the state which gave authority to the police and gave them the power to arrest. Such disobedience can amount to court action against that person. It is the same in the spirit realm. Christians are God's police force; we are his ambassadors, and Satan has no right to disobey us or else he will be charged before the heavenly court, which is a place he does not want to appear. Has anyone been able to mention the name of Jesus in a dream when all forces of darkness surrounded them? Have you experienced the power in that name? What happens at the mention of Jesus thrills me! Every power of darkness disappears at the mention of His name. He is the "name above every name. At the name of Jesus, every knee should bow, of things in heaven and on earth and under the earth, and every tongue acknowledge that Jesus Christ is Lord, to the glory of God the Father" (Philippians 2:9-11).

One of the tricks the Devil uses to cause problems in the home, work place, and in the church, is that he disguises himself to take the face of someone around you. He then uses that disguise to attack you in your dreams, pretending to be the person whose face he stole. Any Christian who is not spiritually-developed and who does not have a gift of discernment would believe this type of dream. Lacking in spiritual discernment might cause you to avoid the person that attacked you in the dream in real life, or to treat that person with suspicion. Ask yourself: what is Satan trying to do? His only weapon is confusion. The Devil knows what the Bible says in James 3:13-18:

> *¹³Who is wise and understanding among you? Let them show it by their good life, by deeds done in the humility that comes from wisdom. ¹⁴But if you harbor bitter envy and selfish ambition in your hearts, do not boast about it or deny the truth. ¹⁵Such "wisdom" does not come down from heaven but is earthly, unspiritual, demonic. ¹⁶For where you have envy and selfish ambition, there you find disorder and every evil practice.*
> *¹⁷ But the wisdom that comes from heaven is first of all pure; then peace-loving, considerate, submissive, full of mercy and good fruit, impartial and sincere.¹⁸Peacemakers*

CHAPTER 7: DREAMS AND VISIONS

who sow in peace reap a harvest of righteousness.

Satan cannot hinder your blessings, but he will set a trap for you to become his prey by causing you to act against the Word of God. Once he has convinced you to disobey God, your own actions will open the door to Satan's visitation.

A lady shared with me how she had dreamt that her mother-in-law had bewitched her. When she woke up from sleeping she became frightened and shared the terrible dream with her husband. Her husband flared up and asked her what made her think that his mother has become a witch. Besides that, how could his own mother bewitch his wife to the extent that she could not bear a child?

The dream sparked up big troubles in their home. So much so that the love and peace that existed before flew out the window. To the lady's astonishment, her husband reported the incident to his mother, and the home was thereby turned into battlefield.

Satan achieved his aim in this situation. The quarrel spread like cancer. Their church was affected and the couple forgot they were Christians. They fought like unbelievers, exposing and disgracing one another.

What that particular lady needed was wisdom and discernment of the spirit. Not everyone has a spirit of discernment, but the right thing to do is to ask God whether a dream was from him or not. If the dream was truly from God, he would confirm it through his Word. Satan does not have the power to confirm anything through Scripture, although he can quote it to you.

There was a day I dreamt about something that did not settle well in my spirit. When I woke, I prayed and asked God for confirmation. However, Satan quoted a scripture to me instead. When I turned to Scripture, I realised that there was no such verse in that particular chapter of the Bible! I became mad at the Devil and I wondered why Satan would quote a scripture to me. Then I heard the Lord say to me, "Mark that voice. Read John 10." I then noticed that Satan did not speak to my inner-self, but rather spoke to me from in a spirit realm.

From that day onward whenever a scripture is given to me to read, I ask for confirmation that the scripture came from God.

Sometime in January of 1993, I had a dream that our Toyota Carina car was stolen. When I woke up, I laughed at the Devil and reminded him that he could not do it. I purposed in my mind to take the matter up in prayer at another, more convenient time. Then one day I forgot to lock the back door of our car when I dropped our son off at school. As I was praying, the Holy Spirit reminded me to go check the car doors. I instantly rebuked the Devil and yelled at him, casting him out of the room and commanded him never to disturb my prayers again. A gentle voice reminded me to just go check the doors; it told me that I had left the back door unlocked. At the second command, I rounded up my prayers and went outside to find the door of the car unlocked. I got back at the Devil and laughed at him scornfully. I said, 'Is that all you can do, and is that what you've been planning? Well, you've lost! You've been exposed."

That same evening, we went to visit a lady at the hospital and I repeated the same mistake of not locking the back door. Again, I rebuked the Devil because he had failed, and I concluded that this must have been the meaning of my dream.

The next time I was praying a thought came to me to pray about our car, but I discarded the thought. My impression at the time was that the battle was all over, that the enemy had been exposed and nothing would happen to the car. Four weeks later the car was stolen from where it was parked by our house.

I was lured into believing that everything was over. If only I had continued to cover the car with the blood of Jesus! The car was stolen at a time we needed it most, during our church anniversary crusade. The handbills for the crusade were in the car. The Devil's plan was to foul up the meeting. But, God took control of the entire situation. The crusade was wonderful! Many souls were saved and some became our new members. My ordination service, which was also scheduled for the same day, went beautifully well. The Holy Spirit took over. He turned our mourning into dancing and made it the best crusade in the history of Dynamic Gospel Ministries International. We did not allow the problem to dominate our thinking: to us, it was as though nothing had happened. We trusted God and He came through for us in His faithfulness.

I encourage Christians to take dreams seriously, no matter how fake or foolish it may seem. Do not disregard it until you have seriously presented it to the Lord in prayer. It does not matter who dreamt; it could be anyone, as long as the person has a spirit, soul, and body, they are entitled to see what's happening in the spirit realm.

Some people see more in the spirit and some hear more things in the spirit than others.

Consider Hosea 4:6-7:

> *My people are destroyed from lack of knowledge. Because you have rejected knowledge, I also reject you as my priests; because you have ignored the law of your God, I also will ignore your children.*
> *⁷The more priests there were, the more they sinned against me; they exchanged their glorious God for something disgraceful.*

CHAPTER 7: DREAMS AND VISIONS

In 1977, I dreamt that someone had taken my brother's name to a witchdoctor in order to terminate his life. As I woke up from the dream, I heard some noisy creatures talking around our house. I woke my dad up, but nobody else heard them. As I prayed, I heard the creatures fly away. The next day, my brother had an accident as he was travelling to Kaduna in Nigeria from our village. As they were driving, a vulture from nowhere hit his windscreen. The windscreen broke and a piece of glass hit him in the back seat. His driver was not hurt. My brother was taken to the hospital and his arm was stitched. I went into fasting and prayer at the time, but did not back up my fasting and prayer with Scriptures. I found it easier to pray than to read the Bible.

God changed a lot of my dreams as I grew with his Word with the help of the Holy Spirit. Dreams come in two ways. An example of one is the dream Joseph had which turned him into his brothers' enemy.

SOME DREAMS ATTRACT SIN

Potiphar's wife was being used by the Devil to tempt Joseph to sin and commit adultery. If Joseph did not run away from that temptation, his dreams would have been eroded and come to nothing.

The Bible tells us to flee every appearance of evil. Compare Joseph's handling of temptation to sin with that of Samson. Unfortunately, Samson submitted to the sin of sexual immorality with Delilah and the result of his sin is recorded forever in history.

VISIONS

Vision-like dreams are insights into the spiritual realm. Visions occur in periods of more awareness of one's environment than with dreams, which usually occur while one is asleep or as a result of tiredness.

God has shown me during my time of worship people being burnt in an underground station. The blaze on that day reminded me about one going to hell. At about 2AM the next morning, the Lord repeated the same vision to me. Without an interpretation of the vision, I became frustrated and began to pray with my friends. After the vision, I took tracts to witness to people at an underground station with the conviction that the vision was about death.

A month later, a friend of mine who worked with the London Fire Department told me that King's Cross had been set ablaze and some people had died. I came to realise that God had shared some of his secrets with me. To the glory of God my intercessory prayer prevented a member of our church from the incident.

WATCH UNTO PRAYER

When I wrote my first book, the Lord showed me a vision of Christians worshipping in church. Then people came into the church with guns and other weapons of war. Those people who entered the church were very angry at the worshipping Christians.

I believe a lot of things will happen at the end. You had better get prepared for the Second Coming of Jesus. The Holy Spirit ministered to me January 1993 about getting prepared. Are you bearing fruits? I pray that you become aware as a Christian about the times we are living in.

WE BELIEVE IN VISIONS

Before we launched our ministry in London, we were already somewhat concerned about the state of Christianity in the United Kingdom. We had pleaded with God to allow us go back to Nigeria, to start the ministry there. Then the Lord showed me a vision when I was praying of white and black people standing in a line trying to get into a church building for worship. And then God said to me: "I will save them in Thousands."

He will save them in thousands as shown in the vision! We have to continue interceding and remind God of the visions He has given to each of us. Satan's kingdom will crumble, to the glory of God!

Dear Reader, let us heed the voice of the Lord, for the time is too short to continue to play games with our lives. Are you ready for Him? He is coming very soon and we need to prepare by cleansing ourselves of every foul and filthy spirit that has hindered us and our forefathers before us.

CHAPTER 8

ORAL SEX IS IMMORAL

Dreams can also attract the Devil to cause a person to be diverted from what God has intended for that individual. Take, for example, the sin of immoral behaviour. Generally speaking, people regard this as a social sin. But what I am talking about here is "oral sex", which is very subtle.

Couples think that it is a private thing to do between partners. However, it is not acceptable by the Holy Spirit. It is the manifestation of a filthy spirit and in the eyes of God is as bad as sleeping with someone else's partner. Oral sex is quite demonic. Remember the aim of these demonic activities is to instigate us to disobey the will of God which leads to God's blessing in our lives.

What was the original plan of God for man and woman as husband and wife? God is our manufacturer and His handbook, the Bible, outlines the way in which man and wife are to experience intimate relations. However, the Devil will always suggest an alternative against God's Will.

In the case of oral sex, using the tongue and/or fingers to cause sexual arousal corrupts Gods standard of lovemaking between a husband and wife. This type of arousal ignores the spiritual aspect of lovemaking which depends upon God to bring about complete satisfaction to both husband and wife. God is the one who prepares the heart to be filled with love for your partner. Oral sex concentrates on stimulating the flesh to the point that the individual loses self-control and ignores the spiritual side of lovemaking. (Remember that self-control is one if the fruits of the spirit.)

There are spiritual consequences connected to the immoral act of oral sex. The ultimate aim of lovemaking between a husband and wife is to conceive a child. However, oral sex creates an avenue for a demonic influence over the child's life. Remember that the same fingers used for this immoral act will then be used to bless another, and the same fingers that are lifted up in worship to God, and are used in the laying on of hands and also to eat. Ask yourself: is this a good practice? Should it be this way?

There was a lady minister who experimented with oral sex a long time ago. That night God visited her. When He came to her, He saw strips of cloth strewn all over the room. He asked this minister what those strips signified, and then told her that those strips of cloth represented filth. It was as if He had come to make an inspection of her house and found that it was not in proper order. She had submitted to that fact by the time she finished cleaning up the mess cause by her immoral act. By then, the Lord had already gone ahead to visit other homes. He came to point out the excess baggage that His people were carrying as a result of momentary pleasure.

Please note that any child conceived within this time could become homosexual or lesbian in practice because the parents opened the door to the Devil. (See, Romans 1:18-32 and 1Corinthians 5:1-13.)

CHAPTER 9

HOW TO KEEP AND MAINTAIN YOUR DELIVERANCE

God can use a man or woman of God to cast out the demons in your life or to minister deliverance to you, but you must be able to keep your deliverance by studying the Bible. Understanding the Bible will reveal who you are in Christ Jesus. It is the spiritual road which will keep your spirit alive. You are a spirit that has a soul and lives in a body. To be able to fight the Devil who is also a spirit, you must know your authority as a child of God.

THE SPIRITUAL RULES THE PHYSICAL

Ephesians 1:3: "Praise be to God and Father of our Lord Jesus Christ, who has blessed us in the heavenly realms with every spiritual blessing in Christ."

You may feel sick in your natural body but the truth is that, when you prayed the Word of God concerning your healing as in 1Peter 2:24, you become healed in the spirit. But you must continue to thank God for his infallible, uncorrupted Word, until your natural body agrees with your spirit being. It is then that you will feel the manifestation of your healing in your body. You should not be moved by what you see, what you hear and feel, but only be moved by the Word of God. Praise the Lord!

When you cannot sleep because of the attack of the enemy, do not get up to worry about it. Do not start confessing negative words, but use that time to worship and praise God. That is that time to begin to get into the Word! You will notice that you will begin to feel sleepy. The Devil would not allow you to study the Bible because he knows the more you study the more knowledge you will acquire to defeat him.

When you pray, do not concentrate on yourself and your family, but intercede for other Christians, pray the will of God to be done here on earth as it is in heaven. Pray for the government and the land you are in, that you may live a peaceable life (1Timothy 2:1-6).

WHY DO SOME PEOPLE REFUSE OR RESIST REVELATIONS?

The god of this world has blinded the eyes and understanding of some in order to hinder them from knowing the truth that will deliver and heal them. Jesus said in Luke 4:18 that He came to preach the gospel to the poor. Still, spiritual poverty is worse than natural poverty. Those who are spiritually poor cannot understand the things of God. This is why some wealthy people are in bondage and cannot enjoy a peaceful lifestyle. They use all sorts of alternative gimmicks to make themselves happy, but it is all empty and their behaviour is appalling and they end up sinning like dogs. Notwithstanding their position in life, it is only the wisdom of God as revealed in his Word that can set those kinds of people – spiritually poor people - free. According to Proverbs 3:19, only the Word of God can make someone act and behave in a wise and respectable manner: "By the wisdom the LORD laid the earth's foundations, by understanding he set the heavens in place".

There are still some Christians who are bound by ancestral spirits and they refuse total deliverance. The Devil will whisper to them to leave the church through which God has revealed their problem to the Pastor. At the point of breakthrough, they will take offense and move to another church where it will take some time for the Pastor to identify them as members of their church and to hear God on their behalf. They prefer to hide among the crowd.

SPIRIT HUSBANDS/WIVES

How do people get involved with these spirits?
Satan is very subtle. He understands the power of God's covenant and he also understands that God has delivered the earth to the children of men. When God created the earth, He also created Adam and gave him authority and power over all things. Satan deceived Adam and his wife, and took their authority from them. God knew that would happen so he prepared the last Adam—the "Son of Man", Jesus Christ—whom Satan tried to deceive into disobeying God. Satan tempted Jesus as he tempted Eve, but could not succeed. Therefore, Jesus took back the power from Satan and restored it back to man.

Man is the rightful owner of the earth. God, who gave the earth to man, has to operate on earth through man. God has to get the permission from man in order to accomplish His intentions of blessings upon mankind. When God wants to use man, He gets his attention to know Him as God, to listen to Him, depend on Him, to respect, fear, and obey Him as the Almighty God. Man also has to understand the principles of the kingdom of God.

It is, therefore, very important that we understand that only God can solve man's problems. Since God is the Manufacturer, only God understands man's problems and only God has the ability to bless man. It is the intention of God to bless man. Read Genesis 1:28: "God blessed them and said to them, 'Be fruitful and increase in number; fill the earth and subdue it. Rule over the fish of the sea and the birds of the air and over every living creature that moves on the ground.'"

Satan knows and understands that it is only the Almighty God, the Creator of heaven and earth, who can help man and solve man's problems. But Satan will still suggest to men that there is an alternative way to solving his problems in order to lure them into sin. The enemy, Satan, gives a temporary solution to problems so that he might cause men to enter into a covenant relationship with him (Satan).

I will give you two examples:

In the summer of 1994, I conducted a ladies' prayer conference. A young lady was in that conference who was frightened to come out to the conference for prayers. To the glory of God, I observed that. The Holy Spirit told me to call her out for prayers. As I prayed over her, she fell on the floor and began to shake uncontrollably. Suddenly, a man's voice spoke through her and said, "I married her, I married her, I cannot come out of her because we've been in a marriage relationship for many years." She began to roll on the floor like a snake.

When she regained consciousness, I asked her about what had happened. She told me that she had travelled to Africa with her mum when she was young. On getting to Africa, she fell ill with fever. Her mother took her to a witchdoctor who administered a temporary healing to her. The doctor initiated her into a covenant relationship with the demon in question. He gave her a mark on her body, took a sample of her blood, and made some incantations which she did not understand. The fever left her in exchange for the spiritual marriage covenant that the witchdoctor had officiated. Neither the girl nor her mum completely understood what had transpired.

As she grew up, she noticed she had an unusual relationship with a strange man in her dreams. From the power of those dreams, an invisible force began to influence her character. I do not know how she found out, but she did know that she had a spirit husband. She also told me that this husband warned her never to come to my meetings. She insisted that she must come, but he told her that she must under no circumstance come out for prayer. However, the Spirit of God overruled the counsel of the demonic forces.

CHAPTER 9: HOW TO KEEP AND MAINTAIN YOUR DELIVERANCE

Another example of temporary solutions which lead to spirit marriage is that, in 1996, a couple joined our church with their four children. Outwardly, they seemed very fine. Two years later, the Lord made me understand that the lady had some spiritual problems. She identified me first as a pastor with the gift of discernment. She began to tell people that she was afraid of me and did not like me. Her attitude toward me gave me a bit of concern. When I enquired from God, He showed me in a vision where she came to me and said, 'I am sorry.' I wondered what she had done wrong against me. I continued to pray about the vision until one or two ladies came and told me what she had said to them, hinting to them that she was afraid of me.

As I prayed further, the Lord revealed to me where she wore a cowry ankle chain. At a prayer meeting, I announced that I saw a lady wearing some cowry ankle chains and said that such a lady should come out for prayers. She pretended she did not understand what I had just said and didn't come out for prayers. I kept quiet because I could not deliver her until she was willing and ready.

Months later, a woman in the church approached this same lady to be her child's godmother during the child's dedication. Now, I could not allow that to happen because she might transfer the evil spirit to the little baby! I was in a fix because I could not tell the woman whose child was being dedicated about the spiritual nature of this other lady.

As her friend, she might tell her what I said and it could backfire on me. Therefore, I decided to invite this lady's husband and reveal what I had envisioned about his wife.

The husband now told me the full story. According to her husband, all his wife's mother's children before her had died in infancy while being breastfed. When her mother became pregnant with her, people advised her to seek help. She went to a witchdoctor who, through the spirit of divination, told her that her own mother (our church member's grandma) was responsible for killing her children in infancy. Her mother was a witch who gave her grandchildren over to demonic spirits in exchange for her own life. As her grandchildren died mysteriously, their grandma had become younger.

This witchdoctor advised this lady (who was our church member's mother) to live in his house until her daughter was born. This lady at our church was, therefore, born into the witchdoctor's family. The witchdoctor also told the mother that, if the grandma would set her eyes on the little girl, the grandma would be blinded. This happened exactly as he said some years later. If the grandma had not become blind, she would have killed the little girl. During this time, the witchdoctor initiated the little girl (our church member) into witchcraft and had also covenanted her to a spirit husband. As she was growing up, the spirit had claim over her life but he allowed her to get married to her natural husband with certain conditions. One of the conditions was she could only make love to her natural husband for the purpose of bearing children. After she gave birth to her four children, she could not have sex with her natural husband again, no matter how her husband tried to please his wife the reply was always a resounding 'No.'

This lady told me that, whenever she would lie down on the bed with her husband, the spirit husband would lie in between them creating a separation between them. She could see the spirit but the husband could not. The spirit husband influenced her character so much that her natural husband became frustrated, and it ruined their marriage.

The painful thing is that many people, like this lady, do not wish to be delivered and, when they find out that a minister knows about their condition, they get offended and move to another church. The spirit of pride will not allow them to stay and be delivered and set free. They make the man or woman of God feel guilty for nothing because the accusation will be that the message being preached was all about them. They also accuse the minister of making references to their spiritual problem even when it is not so. This is the case even when there is no mention of anyone's name.

SPIRIT WIVES

There are some men with the same spiritual problem as this lady. These men can never be satisfied with their wives. They will not appreciate the wife of their youth. They always think that there is a better woman waiting for them and, in most cases, they go after other men's wives. Their choices have nothing to do with beauty, education, character, or any other qualification. They are simply driven by strong, invisible forces which drive them to have sex with other women. Immorality is their number one priority. They blame everybody and everything but themselves. These men may not have been taken to witchdoctors, but their cases may be the result of their father's immoral lifestyle. A man that is immoral cannot earn respect among genuine Christians. His way of thinking is like that of a foolish man. He may claim to be the head of the family, but a head that does act immorally is like a dog.

By driving him to immorality, the Devil is trying to disgrace and discredit the man. But, the man thinks he is only enjoying some secret love.

SOLUTION

The solution is to hate sin. What you do not hate you cannot change. Whatever you tolerate stays with you. There is no

CHAPTER 9: HOW TO KEEP AND MAINTAIN YOUR DELIVERANCE

excuse that is acceptable other than to take back your God-given authority and power and deal with every act of disobedience to the Word of God. Jesus said, "I have given you authority over every power of the enemy and nothing shall by any means hurt you."

Take authority over every ungodly character. The blood of Jesus is stronger and more powerful than all the demonic assignments sent against you. Remove every involvement with the Devil. Break every covenant you may have knowingly or unknowingly entered into with Satan.

Some of these covenants were entered into ignorantly by the words of your mouth. Some young people promise to marry each other out of infatuation. They would say to each other: 'If I don't marry you, I will never marry anyone else.' Some exchange blood. They grow up and apart and marry someone else. But the initial covenant was not cancelled. However, the result of the covenant is that problems are created in the new marriage relationship. Any individual involved in a covenant like this needs deliverance! The person that entered into the covenant will always remember their first love and will be caught up with thoughts that have nothing to do with their present situation. When old memories of past loves surface, Satan is up to something ugly. The individual will begin to get irritated with their partner and make excuses like 'Oh, I got up on the wrong side of the bed today.' The reality is that the individual got up with the wrong thought.

CONCLUSION

God is cleansing the Church in preparation for his Second Coming and is thereby exposing every filthy attitude, many of which have been passed down through generations by ancestral spirits and generational curses. The shaking has started and everything that needs to be shaken will be shaken! Jesus is coming very soon and He is coming for a church without spot or blemish.

One of the methods God is using to cleanse the church is to restore the ministry of the prophet.

Since 1987, when the Lord first appeared to me, He revealed many things concerning future events, and even exposed the evil characters of some ministers and church people whom the Devil had taken captive to carry out his will. Consider 2 Timothy 2:26: "And they that will come to their senses and escape from the trap of the Devil, who has taken them captive to do his will."

Before the Lord Jesus appeared to me, I was often tormented by the spirit of fear. I never lived on my own before I got married. Many ministers had prayed for me about this but nothing happened and even my husband used to take me to other people's homes whenever he was going to be out of the house.

However, after the Lord appeared to me, fear left immediately and I was able to say to myself, 'If Jesus is so real, who then can come into my house and kill me?' The truth of that statement really set me free from the bondage of Satan.

Ancestral spirits and generational curses are responsible for setbacks that people experience in their lives. The perfect will of God is to set us free from the bondage of the Evil One. The Bible in John 10:9 says the Devil comes to steal, kill, and destroy. That is what he comes into people's lives to do. But verse 10b says that Jesus came that we may have life and have it more abundantly.

A word of warning: you should refrain from visiting graveyards. You have no relationship with dead parents and relations. God is a God of the living and not the dead. Visiting the grave of a departed loved one can attract the spirit of a necromancer. Once a person dies, a separation has taken place until you meet them in heaven (if they died in Christ). If they did not die in Christ, their spirit will go to

CONCLUSION

Hell, which is not your portion, in Jesus' name.

Abundant life is your portion, in the name of Jesus. Refrain from every appearance of evil. There is so much power in the spoken word. Every Christian should know that life and death are on the tip of their lips. When I collapsed on April 1, 2005, I went into a coma and was in Intensive Care for over five days. The doctors gave me two weeks to live unless they removed the abscess which they had found in my liver. I was diagnosed a diabetic and my blood count was 500 when the normal rate should be 200. The diabetes affected my eyesight terribly and I also had pneumonia. I ran a high temperature which was difficult to control and the doctors had given up on me and told me that I should say goodbye to my family.

But Papa Jesus, the Great Healer, had not given up and healed me completely! Jesus healed me because I confessed him publicly before the six specialists who had predicted my death. I declared that I would not die but live to proclaim the goodness of the Lord. I further reminded them that I could not die because I was a TV Evangelist who preaches the power of the resurrected Jesus. Besides all this, I had witnessed great healings take place in our own ministry and fully believed that the Lord would heal me.

The truth is that the Lord had already spoken to me on the previous Sunday, March 27, 2005, and had given me

Proverbs 13:2-3: "From the fruit of his lips a man enjoys good things, but the unfaithful have a craving for violence. He who guards his lips guards his life, but he who speaks rashly will come to ruin."

God warned me that I controlled the outcome of my illness by the words that I spoke out of my lips. So I made sure that I did not say anything negative about my illness, and PRAISE GOD he delivered me by his amazing grace!

You see, my illness was another manifestation of evil ancestral spirits and generational curses. My mother had fallen ill at the same age when she was alive and the enemy of my soul was trying to repeat the pattern in my life. When I collapsed, I knew that it was a spiritual attack because I kept seeing the faces of dead people. They would attack me in my dreams and tell me that if I stopped disturbing them (i.e. if I stopped praying against the demonic influences in people's lives), they would leave me alone. By faith, I purchased a white t-shirt in the spirit realm and wrote the words "THE BLOOD OF JESUS THAT SET ME FREE" on the back. I did this because I had seen a vision where those words were written on the hospital wall. It was that act of faith that saved me.

This was not the first time the enemy had tried to establish a generational curse in my life. In 2003, when I travelled to Ghana, as soon as the plane landed the Devil told me that I would die. Then, when I travelled to Pastors house, I tripped, badly hurting my right leg in exactly the same place where my mother had hurt her leg at the same age. In fact, as a result of that fall my mother suffered a limp until she died. However, look for yourself at what the word of God says in 1 Peter 1:17-18.

I had to remind myself that I was born-again and a Minister of God. I prayed and pleaded my cause with God. I prayed that whatever had afflicted me would return to its sender and the pain in my foot left would be taken from me. I had to separate myself from the tradition that was trying to establish itself in my family. I was the first female graduate in my family and the first born-again Pastor in my entire town. I had to make a stand and declare that old things are passed away.

(Too often we allow the traditions, beliefs, and values of our forefathers to cause the Word of God to be of no effect. Remember the example of the outcasts in Chapter 1 of this book.)

How can a person be deemed stupid because of their colour? Who said women should not preach? Our parents and older relatives tell us stories about the ghosts of dead grandparents when we are young to try to establish their traditions in our life, but we have been called to make a stand for Jesus. God is not a respecter of persons and we do not have to live according to the dictations of ancestral spirits and generational curses.

It is vitally important that you remember not to make negative confessions and repeat negative dreams. You will have what you say! Confession brings possession. When you believe God for something, you should look up the corresponding scripture and confess the word of God over your situation until you receive the desired result. Ponder this. It is a spiritual law and the Devil knows it well. He will give you a negative dream because he knows that if you agree with that dream by repeating it, you will have what you say.

Say for example, you have been prayed for in the area of eating in your dream, or in the ending of an intimate relationship with a spiritual husband or wife, but you then have a dream where you are eating or sleeping with that spiritual spouse again. What should you do? I tell you what you should NOT do. Do not fall into the trap of the ancestral spirit and generational curses by believing the dream and repeating what happened in the dream to others. These spirits will use negative dreams to get you to continue the negative behaviour pattern they have established in your family.

Once you have believed God and been prayed for, the matter is over. The only things you need to do upon receiving another negative dream are to rebuke and refuse the dream and then continue to thank God for your deliverance. Consider my earlier testimony about when I believed God for giving me my daughter. If I had repeated the dream and spoken about having a miscarriage, I would have had what I had said. However, it is not only necessary to avoid negative confessions, but you must also confess the correct word over the situation.

Consider this: later, when my daughter was born, I had a dream that I was trying to cross a river with the baby. I saw a false brother who came to snatch the baby. I began to tell this brother about how I had been the fastest runner when I was at school, I even quoted "Greater is he that is in me than he that is in the world," but this was the wrong scripture. It was not until I quoted that "we are more than conquerors through Christ that loved us" that I heard angels cheering and rejoicing in heaven.

Remember my vision about the demon affecting businesses? You must be specific when you quote the word of God or rebuke a demon! In that case, I needed to rebuke the demon of poverty.

Finally, dear Friend, hold your tongue and mind what you say. Do not get concerned about what people say about you. What another person says has no power over you. It is not what a person says that is important; it is what you do with what they say that counts. Value God and treasure His word. When God gives you a scripture, write it down with the date and the time next to it. The scripture that I used to fight my spiritual battles were all given to me by God. Even when I was in the hospital I asked the people that came to visit me to read the scriptures that I had been given by the Lord. This was the only time that I was able to sleep because the spirit that caused my illness would go away upon hearing those scriptures read. Now and then they try to come back one at a time, but I continue to fight them with the word of God. I encourage you to continue to fight with the word of God also, no matter how long the battle seems. Persistence is the key.

Understand who you are in Christ - you are God's masterpiece created for good works!

May God continue to multiply you as you obey him, in Jesus' name.

(All scriptures were taken from the New International Version except where stated otherwise.)

PRAYER OF SALVATION

I truly believe that, as you have read and studied this book, the Almighty God will have revealed to you the very source of your problems. Remember that **God reveals to redeem.** If you were an unbeliever when you started reading this book and God touched you after reading and revealed where your problem is coming from, pray the following prayer:

Dear Father God,
I believe that I am a sinner; I also believe that you sent your son Jesus Christ to die in my place, to reconcile me back to you. I believe in my heart that you raised him from the dead. I confess with my mouth that Jesus is my Lord and Master.

I believe that from now on I am born-again. I can no longer be condemned. Thank you, Jesus. I believe that you are able to take care of what concerns me.
In Jesus' name,
Amen.

PRAYER OF RENUNCIATION

Pray the following prayer to finish the work that God has begun in your life. Remember that the fervent effective prayer of the righteous avails much. The cursed did not come overnight, nor will they leave that way. You have need of patience so that you can receive the promise once you have done the will of God (Hebrews 10:36). You need to pray without ceasing until every curse is uprooted.

Dear Father God,
In the name of Jesus, I renounce every covenant entered into knowingly or unknowingly, whether by my forefathers or my parents on my behalf. I ask for forgiveness and from today onwards I will eat by faith. Whatever I am offered to eat, I will present it to you Lord, bless it, and eat it with thanksgiving.

(If you have ever received a razor incision and/or a native doctor has taken your blood and placed indelible ink in the cut, you have entered into a covenant and should repeat the following:

I use the blood of Jesus to cancel and renounce any covenant entered into through this mark and send the ministering angels to go and uproot whatever evil was done as a result of me receiving this mark. Whatever the enemy has buried or thrown into a river to establish an evil covenant, I loose angels to go and destroy that thing in the name of Jesus.

Lord, any covenant that I have entered into as a result of receiving tattoo's and body piercings, I cancel it in the name of Jesus and I break every bond of slavery connected with this tattoo/body piercing.

Lord, regarding any bodily marks that I have received on my body that have opened the door to the enemy, I plead the bold name of Jesus over them and declare every door which I opened to the enemy closed, in the name of Jesus.

Any covenant that I have entered into which is against the will of God, I renounce it, in the name of Jesus.

I believe that I have been set free by the blood of Jesus. Any mark of ill-luck, I uproot it now, in the name of Jesus.

PRAYER OF RENUNCIATION

From today I receive favour from man and from God. The days of struggling and unnecessary hardship are renounced and cancelled in the name of Jesus Christ.)

From now on I will walk and move in boldness. Thank you, Father, for hearing this prayer.

In Jesus' precious name,
Amen.

AUTHOR CONTACT INFORMATION

Felicia Ifeoma Chidike
Faith Revival Ministries International
52 Lovelace Road
East Dulwich, LONDON
SE21 8JR

E-mail us: revfeliciachidike@yahoo.co.uk
Web: www.faithrevivalministriesinternational.org
Tel: 07454007297